Marcel
Matt Goodman
Alex Gregory
Marcellus Hall
Todd Hanson
Damian Kulash, Jr.
Sam Lipsyte
Rick Marin
Tom McCarthy
Jason Nash
David Rees
Rodney Rothman
Andy Selsberg
Tom Shillue
Paul Simms
Eric Slovin
Dan Vebber

ACCLAIM FOR THE NATIONAL BESTSELLER
THINGS I'VE LEARNED
FROM WOMEN WHO'VE DUMPED ME

"With mini-essays from famous comedians and writers, this book is organized into short chapters of truth, testimonies, and realizations . . . Whether the men pathetically recall their failed dating attempts or are celebrating their record number of 'dumps' as learned experiences, these witty, comical approaches to being dumped are sure to entertain."

—*Publishers Weekly*

"Refreshing, enjoyable . . . a brilliantly free-ranging, form-shifting slice of pop bliss."

—*Buffalo News*

more . . .

"True, poignant, rueful, and, in places, fanciful and even funny tales . . . will resonate with anyone who has ever known longing or heartbreak."
—*Montreal Gazette*

"You expect funny when the driving force behind a book was also a driving force behind *The Daily Show with Jon Stewart* and *The Colbert Report*. Ben Karlin, former exec producer of both, doesn't disappoint."
—*San Diego Union-Tribune*

"No-nonsense, sometimes crass, always amusing lessons."
—*Florida Times-Union*

"A mighty fine read . . . holds its own in the complicated world of attraction and heartbreak . . . You might even acquire a more favorable opinion of the male heart."
—*Columbus Ledger-Enquirer* (GA)

"Some very funny essays by a group of erudite men who are all too familiar with the words 'so long, loser.'"
—*Sacramento Bee*

"At times laugh-out-loud funny and at other times heartbreakingly sad . . . a book that eventually says one thing: You'll survive . . . If you're spending Valentine's Day alone—by choice or by fate, or if you've ever had your ego flattened by a scorning paramour, you'll want to read this . . . A book to love."
—*North Andover Eagle-Tribune* (MA)

"Painfully hilarious breakup stories from some of the funniest people in America."
—*Geek Monthly*

Things I've Learned From Women Who've Dumped Me

Edited by
Ben Karlin

Additional Editing by
Andy Selsberg

GRAND CENTRAL
PUBLISHING

NEW YORK   BOSTON

Compilation copyright © 2008 by Ben Karlin
Introduction copyright © 2008 by Ben Karlin

Page 224 constitutes an extension of the copyright credits information.

Grand Central Publishing
Hachette Book Group
237 Park Avenue
New York, NY 10017

Visit our Web site at www.HachetteBookGroup.com.

Printed in the United States of America
Originally published in hardcover by Grand Central Publishing.

First Trade Edition: January 2009
10 9 8 7 6 5 4 3 2 1

Grand Central Publishing is a division of Hachette Book Group, Inc.
The Grand Central Publishing name and logo is a trademark of Hachette Book Group, Inc.

The Library of Congress has cataloged the hardcover edition as follows:

Things I've learned from women who've dumped me / edited by Ben Karlin. — 1st ed.
     p. cm
  Includes bibliographical references.
  ISBN: 978-0-446-58069-4
  1. Man-woman relationships—Case studies. 2. Rejection (Psychology)—Case studies.
3. Separation (Psychology)—Case studies. 4. Sex (Psychology)—Case studies. I. Karlin, Ben
  HQ801.A2T45 2008
  306.7081—dc22

                                 2007037697

ISBN 978-0-446-69946-4 (pbk.)

Book design and text composition HRoberts Design

This one's for the ladies

"Time heals some wounds."
—**American folk saying**

Contents

Foreword

I Think My Son Is a Catch

by Barbara Karlin

My son is a real catch and shame on any girl who's ever thought otherwise.

He's tall, but not too. He runs marathons and scales mountains. And of course he has those gorgeous blue eyes. And on top of it all, he's funny. Of course I didn't think everything he did was so funny when he was a kid. I used to tell him "that's not so funny" all over the house. Back then I called him a smart aleck but now I call him "creative." If you make money from being a smart aleck, you're creative. If you don't make money, you're a putz. So, he's creative. Come on, girls, why would you break up with my creative son?

And a good time he'll show you. You want fine restaurants? My Benjamin knows them all—and he isn't afraid to spend his money. Not on me of course, but that's not what I'm here to talk about. You want travel and adventure? He's been all over the world. Without me. A great communicator you want? Well, I know he'll call you more than he calls me. You want someone who can sing and dance? Forget about it.

Catches like my Benjamin you don't find every day. Did I mention he can cook? I'm not talking brisket or chicken soup. I'm talking very fancy food I've never heard of. He'll make things so pretty you won't know whether to eat them or wear them.

And then he makes these funny little jokes about you not appreciating it on the same "level" as he does. I'm not sure what that means. But if you want to try organic fiddlehead ferns, he's your man.

Whenever a girl would dump my son—and he had his share of heartbreak as a boy—I would always say the same thing to him: "Those girls are all fools and idiots. They don't know what they're missing." He would always say, "You're just saying that because you're my mom." He had me there.

But I'd like to think just because he's my son, and I gave birth to him and fed him from my breast and raised him, doesn't mean I can't look at things objectively. Sure I can! I guess you can tell how much I love my son and what a great catch he is. So if you catch him, please tell him to call his mother.

Introduction

by Nick Hornby

At the time of writing, I have been happily married for thirteen months, to a woman I have been living with for eight years. Thanks to the book you are currently holding in your hand, the implications of this are now clear to me: not only have I learned nothing whatsoever for the best part of a decade, but also the things I did learn are beginning to fade disastrously from the mind, in much the same way that the five or six facts gleaned from my formal education have almost disappeared. (I used to pride myself on being able to remember three of the Chartists' six demands, but the three, I now realize, have become one: universal suffrage. That must have been a big one, though, right? The other five were surely all minor disgruntlements, by comparison.)

No, instead, reading about all this learning reconciles me to the future, when I have messed this marriage up and I'm back on the singles circuit, aged fifty-nine, say, or sixty-seven, or eighty-two; the success of institutions like the University of the Third Age demonstrates that our thirst for learning remains unquenched even in our twilight years.

It is perhaps best not to analyse too closely what exactly it is that these writers have gleaned from their romantic mishaps. Andy Selsberg, for example, has clasped to his bosom the lesson that holding grudges is fun. (Well, der! What did he think relationships were for? Mutual support, raising children, looking after each other in old age? And how old are you, Andy?) Rodney Rothman learns that the girl who broke his heart doesn't actually remember dating him in the first place. Dan Savage found out that he wasn't interested in women. This is all useful stuff, but one can see that anyone doubtful about the intellectual value of romantic trauma might still need a little more evidence of its efficacy.

What strikes one about these essays is that many of the authors seem to have found contentment in their relationships *since*, and there is a suggestion implicit in the book's title that through dumping came wisdom, and through wisdom domestic bliss. I'm not so sure. A good, if tasteless, comparison (but one I am allowed to make because of my nationality) is with Londoners during the Blitz: did bombs stop dropping on us because we had somehow learned enough to prevent them from dropping? I would argue not. I would argue that other factors, too complicated to go into here (but see Winston Churchill, *The Second World War*, volumes two and three), were responsible. The major, but vital, contribution of Londoners was their refusal to let their morale be broken by the relentless bombings. And then, one day in May 1941, the Germans took their firepower elsewhere.

Well, isn't that it? It seems that the major, but vital, contribution of men to the war of attrition that takes place between the ages of thirteen and about thirty-five, if you're lucky, is our refusal to let our morale be broken. Cheese-eating surrender monkeys would open a packet of char-grilled steak-flavored peanuts, crawl under our sports-themed duvet covers, and stay there until we were certain that the last sparks of sexuality had withered and died. We didn't do that, mostly because we were too stupid. We ignored the air-raid wardens and ran up and down the streets waving torches.

In those formative years, we got creamed, mashed, pissed on (I'm speaking figuratively here, but there are, of course, some people who like that sort of thing, and it's not my intention to judge them); we got told we were stupid, feckless, reckless, scared, boring, unserious, too serious, too bookish, nerdy, unattractive, too drunk, too stoned, too sporty, too couch-potatoey, too out-doorsy, too political, too insular, too angry, too drippy, too suspi-cious, too complacent, too ambitious, not ambitious enough, too poor. I know I got told that, anyway. (I'll bet you that somebody, somewhere, got told he was too handsome, too successful, too kind, too thoughtful, and too good in bed.)

It is only fair to point out that we gave as good as we got during this time. We sent the RAF out there night after night to cheat, lie, and refuse to commit. Most of the people in this book, creative types all, were refused admission on medical grounds, although I suspect the contributors who were in bands were involved in some of the terrible carpet-bombing that went on during the twenties. (Indeed, some of the zeal shown by our fellow males made some of us feel a little queasy.) There were no winners, and there was nobody who could seize the moral high ground. And then one day, maybe even one day in May, it stopped. We woke up in the morning, went to a bar or a party or onto the Internet, and somebody there liked us, and married us, and there was a new dawn of peace, prosperity, and babies.

Cynics might say that last word had a great deal to do with what happened. Cynics might say these beautiful, fantastic women who have taken us on actually looked at us a few years ago, found us wanting, and have since come back to us, having argued themselves into believing that, actually, we aren't that bad, all things considered. I married the one who dumped you, and you married the one who dumped me, but that's the story. Effectively we become the DVD of *Elf* that you ignore in the rental store at nine o'clock on a Friday night, on the presump-tion there will be something better (or at least, something more fulfilling, more complex, and that you haven't seen twice before) on the shelves somewhere. And guess what you end up going home with? Well, that's what we are to these beautiful, fantastic women: Elves.

Here are the titles of some e-mails my wife has sent me in the past few months: "Event reminder: The Wiggles"; "Catering Menu"; "Joint a/c"; "Various boring"; "New plans for car tax"; "Fishcakes??"; "No fishcakes"; "Fishcakes?!" E-mail hadn't been invented when I was suffering the slings and arrows of outrageous Miss Fortune, of course. But if it had, I would never have believed that anybody for whom I had any kind of romantic feelings would communicate with me in this way. In life during wartime, there were neither fishcakes nor no fishcakes, and e-mails would have titles like "Sorry," "Last night," "My relationship with Michael," "My actual relationship with Michael," and "You bastard." These might sound more interesting than the various borings, but they weren't, not really, because they became life itself; there were no children, of course, but there wasn't much else, either. I never had the time or the concentration to write books, and I never even had the time or the concentration to read them, either. Everything was focused on trying to get my romantic life right, and that turned out to be precisely the way to get it disastrously wrong. I get e-mails about fishcakes because there's absolutely nothing to say about the other stuff: it just *is*, day after day, and that seems like a miracle. You get a lot more done during peacetime; you even get a love life thrown in.

Lesson #1   Sex Is the Most Stressful Thing in the History of the Universe

by Dan Vebber

When I was a child, sex was awesome. Of course, when I was a child, I didn't have to deal with it. Sex was what Dan of the Future would one day enjoy, and I saw no reason to obsess about it any more than Present-Day Dan obsesses with . . . what's something old people enjoy? Nice breezes? Let's say nice breezes.

In fact, I never beat off as a kid. I didn't beat off thinking about girls, I didn't beat off thinking about boys, I didn't even beat off thinking about spaceships. (This is the point at which people quote me HILARIOUS statistics along the lines of "99 percent of teenage boys masturbate, and one percent are liars!" HA! Thank you for your opinion, please return to hosting your Morning Zoo program.) The fact is, not once during my outwardly normal adolescence could I dupe my machinery into getting physically aroused by the mere thought of sex, the touch of my own hand, or porn. (Not every guy has a long-standing and storied relationship with porn. Some of us honestly don't find it interesting enough to warrant looking past the girls' bad teeth.)

When I was seventeen, I started dating Molly Malone. I've changed her name here, but not her full-blooded Irish ethnicity or any of the attendant baggage that implies. Catholic? Check. Shocking red hair and freckles? Check. Overbearing, shillelagh-waving father? Double check. Our senior year of high school, Molly and I were inseparable, and at least as far as the sex thing went, we were perfect for each other: She didn't want to lose her virginity because of her Catholic guilt, and my retarded libido wasn't compelling me to pressure her into it. She was my first real love, breaking through my veneer of irony and cynicism to the point where I actually enjoyed squiring her to a prom with the odious theme "Knights in White Satin."

Molly was a brilliant girl, and translated that brilliance into acceptance to no less of a prominent Ivy League institution than Havrard University. (I have flipped the third and fourth letters of the school's name to further protect identity.) This is where things started to fall apart, as Molly became increasingly obsessed with the notion that she, with her love of deconstructing wordplay in French poetry, was much smarter than me, with my love of deconstructing the comedic premise behind David Letterman wearing a suit made of Alka-Seltzer. One night we were making out and listening to XTC's "The Mayor of Simpleton," the lyrics of which are a plea from an idiot to a brainy girl along the lines of "I may not be well versed in any topics that would gain me admiration among the intelligentsia, but the one thing I DO know is that I love you." Delighted, Molly pointed out to me, "Aww, it's a song about us!" At the time I took the comment in the spirit of playfulness that was likely intended. But years later, looking back . . . Jesus! What the fuck was that? More importantly, what the fuck was wrong with ME that I was so willing to put up with a girlfriend who repeatedly hammered into my head that I was a dumb-ass?

Being a brainless troglodyte, I ended up in Madison at the University of Wisconsin. My existence became an endless blur of dorm-room keggers, advocacy journalism, and focusing my abnormally large reserves of vitriol on fellow students dumb enough to be vexed by the question, "But is it art?" Clarity only seemed possible during the times when Molly and I would visit each other. As these dorm-room visits were the first time we had access to unsupervised beds, we'd spend a lot of time sleeping together. Though for us "sleeping together" was merely the next logical step on our path toward sexual intercourse, as opposed to a euphemism for it. The mere insertion of parts into other parts would have seemed anticlimactic after an evening spent solving the Gordian knot of balancing two sleeping bodies on a single mattress, waking up with severely restricted blood flow in at least one limb, and overlooking each other's post-Chinese-food morning breath.

As magical as those visits with Molly were, the time spent apart from her became that much more unbearable. This wasn't helped by the fact that Molly was acting totally unreasonably at her new school, engaging in conversation with guys who weren't me and attempting to join social groups that weren't made up of me, me, and me. On some Friday nights she would even choose to attend a book club or act in a play rather than sit alone by her phone waiting for my sobbing call. How could one girl be so heartless?

Our dance of dysfunction and lack of sex continued throughout our freshman and sophomore years. We called the whole thing off more times than I can remember, and usually for reasons that were entirely my fault. The ratio of time spent long-distance dating to time spent long-distance broken up gradually decreased, until we agreed to acknowledge what geography had been screaming at us for months: we were no longer together.

The spring of 1991, my junior year, was an exciting time. I had a dorm room to myself, I was drawing a well-regarded daily comic strip for my school paper, and Our Troops had just finished kicking Saddam's ass in the first Gulf War, setting the stage for the peace in the Middle East we enjoy to this day. I had moved on from Molly and was a better man for it, though my inexperience with sex was starting to be a problem. The girls I dated wanted more than a smooch and a boob kneading to top off their night. "We should wait until we're ready," I'd declare, usually succeeding in convincing potential partners that I was a sensitive and decent man as opposed to a tragically repressed and inexperienced boy. The problem with this tactic was that a girl, once flattened by my tsunami of sensitive decency, would fall for me even harder, making it that much more difficult to dump her when my well of excuses for putting off sex finally ran dry. Their faces haunt me to this day: the suburban punker who worked the counter at the record store, the doe-eyed lifeguard certified in massage, the perky art chick who scraped up roadkill and used it in an installation piece . . . They were nerdy goddesses all, young and horny, but I could never make a relationship with them last more than a couple weeks and I was starting to hate myself for it. Such was my state of mind when Molly called me out of nowhere and requested I fly to Boston for the express purpose of having sex.

The specific circumstances surrounding Molly's offer of virginity loss are admittedly fuzzy, and largely rooted in emotion. But what I do remember with the clarity of tropical fish footage on a Best Buy showroom HDTV is that we were definitely, definitely not in love anymore. Knowing this, I was overcome with the absolute certainty that this "orgasm-or-bust" odyssey could not possibly end in anything but disaster and embarrassment for both of us. I bought the first plane ticket I could find.

Once I arrived at Havrard, Molly and I went straight to work constructing the infrastructure she deemed necessary for "safe sex." This consisted of four forms of birth control, which, per Molly's instructions, would need to be utilized simultaneously.

One: The Rhythm Method

There was a window of three or four days in Molly's cycle that she had calculated to be "safe." That window didn't open until a couple days into my visit, so we killed time, probably walking the Freedom Trail or some shit.

Two: Condoms

We went to purchase these together, studying the boxes until we were confident we'd found the thickest, least comfortable, most spermicide-drenched contraceptives science could produce.

Three: The Sponge

I'm thirty-seven and I still don't know quite how these are supposed to work. More on this later.

Four: The Number-One Rule

"DO NOT ejaculate while inside me! Pull out the second you think it's getting dangerous."

In retrospect, she may not have wanted to get pregnant.

Beginning with her phone call, and throughout our quest to purchase birth control, Molly's constant mantra was, "We've got to get this over with." Is there any sentence in the English language that conveys less passion or romance? Thanks to the last moments leading up to our attempt at sex, Molly provided me with at least one: "Just so you know, this is going to be really painful for me, and I'm probably going to be bleeding all over the place." This final sweet nothing imparted, and the fortress of contraception having been built (including Molly's mood-killing last-minute dash behind a closed bathroom door so she could have privacy as she put the sponge in), it was finally time for me to get a boner and fuck my way into adulthood. Three, two, one . . . go! Go! The light is green! The ref fired his starter pistol! Cut the yellow wire RIGHT NOW or the bomb goes off!

It didn't take Molly long to notice something was up, or more accurately, wasn't. After all, whenever we had gone at it with the unstated understanding that no sex was forthcoming, I'd grow a cop's flashlight in my pants. (My point is not to imply that I have a particularly large penis, but simply to state via colorful metaphor that my boners came more easily when I wasn't picturing Molly bleeding to death.) Molly's reaction to my lack of stiffness was, at first, sympathetic, if confused ("It's okay. Take your time."), but quickly snowballed into impatient, nastier territory ("I'M doing everything right. What's wrong with YOU?"). After a couple futile hours of frustration, hair pulling, and being flat-out belittled by My Wild Irish Rose, I put on my clothes and exited Molly's dorm room into the drizzly Havrard night, alone.

On that walk, I ate half a bag of white-cheddar popcorn and came to the conclusion that would screw me up forever: I was incapable of having sex. Never mind that no one but the randiest of porn stars would have been able to get it up amidst the shitstorm of stress, fear, and inexperience I was dealing with. Such logical explanations were obliterated by my feelings of failure and shame, compounded by Molly's anger that her virginity problem wouldn't be solved anytime soon.

The next night we went to a party, where I embarrassed Molly by conversing with one of her more bearable friends about our shared obsession with the band Devo. "These people go to Havrard! They don't want to talk about stupid shit like Devo!" Molly screamed. I, in turn, exploded at her flat-out wrong assessment of her friend's degree of interest in Akron's proudest sons, and suddenly we were in the fight that ended our relationship once and for all. We agreed to avoid each other over the six remaining days of my trip. (Why I didn't just fly home on an earlier flight is lost to the mists of time, but knowing me, I probably didn't want to inconvenience the airline.) I spent my nights freezing on Molly's couch, and my days reading Vonnegut outside an Au Bon Pain. I think I may have had a nervous breakdown at some point, as I distinctly remember curling up next to Molly's dorm-room fireplace, sobbing uncontrollably about nothing and everything. (And what kind of bullshit dorm room has a fireplace in it, anyway? Fuck Havrard.)

In the end, after all we went through, the most enduring lesson I learned from Molly is that regardless of whether or not my parts work on a given try, sex is always the most stressful thing in the history of the universe. After (and because of) our failed attempt at Sin, it took me three more years to officially lose my virginity. And to this day, despite being blissfully married and having fathered a kick-ass son, I consider myself a victim of Post-Traumatic Sex Disorder. (If I've inadvertently stolen this term from a struggling stand-up comedian, I humbly apologize.) Every single sexual encounter of my life has been preceded by feelings of overwhelming dread, because no matter how many hundreds of times I've hardened up and rocked it in there, part of me is still that confused twenty-year-old, staring at my flaccid shame, getting berated for being defective. Worse still, the mere whiff of white-cheddar popcorn still brings back all the hopeless feelings I went through in the rain that night almost twenty years ago. And I used to love that shit!

I did, however, learn to masturbate at age twenty-four, making me the only man on earth to lose his virginity to a girl before losing it to himself. And if that fact doesn't bring a tear of hope to your eye, then I'm sorry, but you simply aren't human.

Girls Don't Make Passes at Boys with Fat Asses

by Andy Richter

My parents divorced when I was four, and afterwards my brother, mother, and I moved into my grandparents' house, where a particularly bone-crushing form of matriarchal rule was practiced. At first my grandmother protested against having to care for me while my mother worked, and insisted that I be enrolled in the Jack and Jill Nursery School so that I wouldn't cramp her Margaret Dumont of Mayberry lifestyle. Her protests were soon proven to be just a way to fuck with my mother, waste our money, and make a difficult time in my mom's life even more difficult, as most days my grandma kept me out of Jack and Jill and made me her sidekick on an endless round of shopping trips, bridge game lunches, and ladies' auxiliary something-or-others.

On one such excursion, my grandmother and I were in the tearoom of Marshall Field's department store, where we had stopped for a snack. The snack, for me, consisted of a hot fudge sundae, which my grandma asked me if I had enjoyed. After I responded in the affirmative, she asked a question which still chills me.

"Does it taste like *more*?"

There were moments in my childhood where a preternatural maturity rose up in me, where the Future Me would seem to pop through to the surface and say, "Hold on, wait a minute, what's going on here is fucked up." This, however, was not one of those moments. In this moment a fat little boy was given permission by his adult guardian to order a *second* hot fudge sundae, and the fat little boy, being a little boy, said yes. As I tucked into my second sundae, my grandmother smiled, enjoying seeing her grandson made happy. Now, though, I imagine there was more to that smile. I like to think that that smile was a sly wink to all the women who would someday not fuck me, and a fuck-you to all those who might.

Now it is not my intention to get all victimy, as I know just as well as the next guy how to put down a spoon. And I don't really think that the women in my family were conscious of the fact that by overfeeding me they were channeling their aggression towards the women who might someday steal me away. But, while it might not take a whole village, it definitely takes more than one person to make a fat kid. And the fat kid is what I was, with the "husky" jeans, President's Physical Fitness Test dread, and chafing thighs to prove it.

Navigating the waters of adolescent intergender relations is tricky business for even the most psychologically aerodynamic youngster, but doing it with the added weight of added weight is far more conducive to sinking than swimming.

For the longest time I couldn't fathom how a girl could find me attractive, when there were so many other examples of young manhood burgeoning unfettered. And since I was doing such a fantastic job rejecting myself, it seemed redundant to let the local girls get a crack at rejecting me, too. So, except when absolutely necessary (homecoming dances and proms), I didn't date. At the time, and in later therapy sessions, I would put this down to being the product of two divorces; to being so shell-shocked by the dissolution of my parents' marriage and my mother's subsequent one, that any attempt at a romantic relationship was so deadly important and fraught with eventual domestic doom that I would just rather sit on the sidelines and watch the other kids play the game. Looking back, however, I think a stronger contributing factor to my inaction was simply the fear of having to take my clothes off in front of somebody. Luckily, at some point in college, biology won out and I realized that if I didn't cut out this self-loathing bullshit I was never going to get laid. And to my surprise, I was very good at getting naked. A genius, even. God bless artsy girls and booze!

I am now on the southern end of forty, married, and the father of two, and my weight is what it should be for a man my age, a health concern. This is because of my wife, whose love and affection make me feel safe and secure and give me a place in the world to really be. And while I really do believe in and truly know unconditional love, I don't want to give the impression that my wife is that kind of asshole who will stand by her man no matter how much he messes his spiritual diaper. No, don't get me wrong: if I was to really bloat up, she might very well leave me. Or at least start sleeping around, bless her heart.

And so, aside from wanting to be with my family for as long as I can, my girth, or occasional lack of it, is almost entirely a professional matter. Now that I'm a grown-up it's as if I've somehow transformed my fear of rejection into a career as a rejection junkie, or at least as somebody with a high rejection tolerance. Why would someone with a history of happiness-crippling body issues choose to go into a line of work so heavily focused on appearance? To a job where it seems I can't read for a part unless the script refers to the character as "expansive," or "a bear of a man," or in the better-written scripts, plain old "fat"?

My coping mechanism is fairly simple, and it goes like this: I have brainwashed myself to believe that if they like me, they're geniuses. And if they don't like me, then they're idiots, and I will gather the pearls I have cast before the hopeless, clueless swine and head off to some other sty. This M.O., which really does work for me, most likely comes from an ironic inheritance from dear old Grandma, and that is the firm belief that I am better than almost everybody.

I have even occasionally been a leading man. Well, that is to say, I have been the lead character in a number of television shows. That they are all no longer on the air could be seen as evidence of a mass rejection of me, but I know that it's much more complicated than that. (So many factors contribute to the demise of a show that I can't explore them all here: for the sake of space, let's just boil it down to its essence and say that many of the men and women who run our television networks are gutless cunts.)

No, I have come to believe that people generally seem to like me. I don't think of myself as the sexual untouchable that I once did, although there is actual scientific data showing that men like me better than women. And I like me, too, so I will keep plugging away, fueled by the belief that people will actually pay money to see me, to accept me just as I am.

Although, of course, it wouldn't hurt to drop a few pounds. It almost never does.

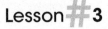

Beware of Math Tutors Who Ride Motorcycles

by Will Forte

Her name was Michelle and she was my first serious girlfriend. We had met at a fraternity party one night and somehow, during the course of that evening—aided no doubt by generous portions of cheap beer—I tricked her into liking me. That first meeting turned into a first date and then another date and then soon, she and I were boyfriend and girlfriend. How had I lucked into this? I was dating an attractive woman who didn't care that I dressed like a slob and had a bowl cut and drank myself into oblivion every third night. It was paradise.

One weekend, I went up to Lake Tahoe for a ski race. After a day of getting my ass handed to me by superior ski racers, I was in a bit of a funk—and there was only one person who could cheer me up: my beloved Michelle. As this was pre–cell phone and the rotary phone at our condo was locked, I convinced the team to drive by the local grocery store pay phone. My call went to her answering machine, but that was okay—I had a plan. I offered Michelle three different times to wait by the phone for a call from me later—8:00, 10:00, and midnight. Satisfied, I jumped in the van and took off for dinner.

After dinner, I convinced the team to swing by the grocery store again. I called Michelle at 8:00 on the nose and once again got her answering machine. No big deal. She was probably at dinner or something. With two-thirds of my calling options still available, I hopped back into the van and headed back to the condo.

I returned to the pay phone at exactly 10:00, dialed Michelle's number, and once again got her answering machine. Again, no big deal. In fact, I should have seen it coming. 10:00? Michelle wouldn't pick 10:00. She'd pick midnight, for sure. She'd want my voice to be the last thing she heard before she went to sleep and dreamed sweet dreams of the two of us sharing our lives together. What a romantic! I walked away from the pay phone, smiling.

By midnight, everyone was pretty drunk. Everyone except me. I mean, somebody had to stay sober enough to drive me to the pay phone. Eventually, a few ski teamers figured out the reason for my sobriety and I caught a considerable amount of shit for it. The general consensus was that "Forte's pussy-whipped!"—a charge I vehemently denied. But deep inside, I knew they were right.

I got to the pay phone at 11:50, had a ten-minute fake phone conversation to fend off any would-be phone users, then finally at midnight, jammed my quarters into the coin slot and dialed. "Ring . . . ring . . . ring . . . ring . . ."

"Hi . . ."

"Michelle?"

". . . this is Michelle. Leave your name and number at the beep." *Beep.*

Fuck. She must be down the hall in the bathroom or something. I hung up and tried again. Again, answering machine. I hung up and waited for five minutes. Again, answering machine. Shit, was she okay? Should I call her parents? Maybe she was in a car accident or a library mugging. Was this a valid 911 situation? Wait, maybe I should commandeer the ski team van and haul ass back down to Los Angeles? Soon, the rational minority of my brain took over the irrational majority and I realized there was probably a very good reason she didn't answer the phone. The next morning, I found out this reason.

"Oh, I went to dinner with friends."

"Thank God. I thought you were hurt or something."

"Sorry, no. It was just a late dinner," she explained. "And then I went out for drinks after that with Steve . . ."

The name Steve hung in the air for what seemed an eternity.

". . . so I didn't get your message until this morning."

Hm. Steve? I'd never heard of "Steve." And they went out for drinks? Alone? I mean, couldn't they have talked some others into joining them? I had so many questions to ask Michelle about Steve, but didn't know how to ask without sounding like an asshole. After a long pause, I finally found the perfect way to word my concerns:

"So . . . uh . . . Steve?"

Michelle sighed, as if she knew I was going to say that. "Relax, Will. We're just friends."

"Hm . . . Okay, that's good enough for me."

It wasn't. As we got off the phone, I wondered about Steve. Was he some tattooed clubber guy? Was he on a collegiate sports team? Would a representative for a modeling agency approach him on the street and give him their card?

I walked back to the van and, in a jealous mini-rage, slammed the door hard enough to provoke a "Trouble in paradise?" comment from one of the ski teamers. *Could be, ski teamer,* I thought to myself. *Could be.*

That night, I slyly asked Michelle all about Steve. I didn't like what I heard. Apparently, Steve was a blond-haired, blue-eyed surfer. He was nice, smart, and funny. But nothing scared me more than the information I found out next: Steve played bass for a popular campus band called the Brewmasters. Oh, great, a fucking musician. When pressed, Michelle admitted that she found Steve attractive, but claimed she didn't think of him in "that way." As I went on with my questions, Michelle became annoyed. Didn't I believe her? They were just friends. Steve was

helping her with her studies. If anything, he should be thanked—
I mean, the more solid grasp she had on her math theorems, the
quicker she would do future math theorem homework, and the
quicker she could meet me for romantic date nights at local taco
establishments.

"Sure. You're right. I'm sorry." But I wasn't sorry. Deep
down, I knew the truth: Steve was not a man to be thanked.
Steve was the enemy. Their friendship had to be terminated, and
it had to be terminated quickly.

I immediately began trying to fill Michelle's calendar with
events. I figured any open time could potentially be "Steve
Time." I'm pretty sure Michelle knew something was up. I had
never been a big planner and here I was suddenly planning 6:45
coffee dates and 9:15 campus strolls. But even during this bar-
rage of scheduling, Michelle carved out a little study time with
Steve—all the while insisting they were just friends.

The next week, Michelle and Steve increased the frequency
of their study dates. I was not happy, but with finals approaching,
I had to admit there was some validity to this "studying" alibi. So
I hunkered down—soon finals would be over and Steve and
Michelle would have nothing more to study. Michelle would be
all mine once more.

During finals week, Michelle and I saw very little of each
other. I was busy learning an entire quarter's worth of history in
a four-day period. She was preparing in her own way, via late-
night cramming sessions with Steve. Michelle called me after
her last final on a Thursday night. She was going out to celebrate
with friends. Would Steve be among those friends? The answer
was yes. I cringed. But there was nothing I could do. I had a history final the next day for which I was hideously unprepared. I
tried to block it all out as I dove into my textbooks. And for a
while, it worked. But then there was a knock at my door.

"Dude, I think I just saw Michelle on the back of some guy's
motorcycle."

I rushed to the window to see Michelle standing next to a motorcycle across the street from my fraternity. I hurried out of the house and ran across the street to her.

"Hey, Michelle, what are you doing here?"

"Steve forgot something at his apartment."

Just then, Steve bounded down the stairs.

"Will, this is Steve."

Steve was incredibly nice:

"Oh hey, man! Great to finally meet you! Michelle told me all about you."

But nice in the way people might be nice when they're having sex with your girlfriend.

"Hi, Steve," was all I could offer. Then we smiled at each other for a long time. Was this as weird for them as it was for me? I had to say something to break the silence.

"So you live up here?"

"Yep."

Steve pointed to his apartment—across the street from my fraternity house. I thought of all the spying I could have been doing the past several weeks. More awkward silence.

"Well, we should get going."

I reluctantly agreed. "Yeah, I should get back to studying."

With that, Steve kick-started his motorcycle and Michelle hopped up behind him. As she reached her hands around his waist, I died inside a little. I walked back to my fraternity, bolstered by the support I got from my brothers.

"Dude, he's totally gonna plow her."

"For your information, he's very good at math and he's helping her with that." I wanted so badly for it to be true I almost had myself convinced.

That night, as I should have been studying, all I could think about was those arms reaching around his waist. I thought of the same thing happening in a bar—her arms reaching around his waist as he was ordering her a fifth Corona. All night, I kept waiting for Steve's motorcycle to pull up across the street. I'd feel so much better when I saw him get back and walk up those stairs to his apartment, alone. But the motorcycle never came. Maybe he parked it somewhere down the street or maybe it broke down somewhere and he walked home that night. Maybe it was totaled when he foolishly tried to jump a hundred parked school buses in the middle of the desert.

The next morning, I went to class, shat out my test, and ran back home to call Michelle. Finally, she answered.

"Will, we need to talk."

And with that, I knew it was over. I went to her apartment and we started the proceedings. The first part of the breakup featured some pre-breakup small talk. (It's bad form to launch directly into the meat of the breakup.) Next came the "airing of grievances" phase in which she listed the problems with our relationship. I have to admit, she made several strong points. Next came the rebuttal phase in which I went through a long list of things I'd be happy to change to make it work. She took this into consideration. Next came the actual breakup. This part was oddly short. And then suddenly we were no longer boyfriend and girlfriend. But there was still one last phase that was very specific to our breakup. I'll call it the "Are you with this Steve guy now?" phase. And this must have lasted like, a half-hour. But she insisted she was not. She and Steve were just friends. And you know what? Maybe she was telling the truth. I had no proof to the contrary. All I had was a mountain of circumstantial evidence and a very strong hunch. We parted ways.

That night, while everyone was celebrating the end of the quarter, I just sat in my room, alone. After several hours of wallowing in self-pity, I was interrupted by a knock at the door.

"Dude, Michelle just showed up across the street on the back of some guy's motorcycle."

I ran to the window and sure enough, there were Michelle and Steve, back from God knows where. Why did this guy have to live across the street from me? Hadn't they tortured me enough? I watched Michelle follow Steve upstairs and disappear out of view. I wondered what the hell was going on up there. Were they really just friends? I'd never know.

Or would I?

I grabbed my binoculars and ran from room to room, looking for the perfect vantage point. Finally, on the third floor, I found one—a direct view into Steve's apartment. Sure, the curtains were drawn nearly all the way shut, but there was a two-foot opening that I was able to peer into. That was all I needed. I stared into that window for four solid hours looking for anything—a kiss, a hug, a caress—anything that would prove they were more than what they claimed to be. But I got nothing. Well, okay, not nothing. I saw Michelle walk by the curtain once, fully clothed, and about an hour later I saw Steve walk by, also fully clothed. Eventually I gave up and went down to a bar and got drunk with friends.

The next morning, I saw Michelle walk down the apartment stairs in the same outfit she'd been wearing the night before. She hopped on the back of Steve's motorcycle, reached around his waist, and drove off down the street. Later that day, I called her and told her what I had seen.

"How many times do I have to tell you, we're just friends!"

After that, I would see Michelle leaving Steve's apartment in the morning on a pretty regular basis. And occasionally I would run into her at parties. I would always ask her what was going on with her and Steve. Her story never changed: she and Steve were just friends.

Eventually, I moved on to other failed relationships and forgot all about Michelle and Steve. I did, however, run into Michelle a year ago at a store in New York. She's doing great: mother of three and happily married to . . . Steve.

There's an old bit of kitchen wisdom that says you should always marry your best friend. Well, to this day, I can't think of anyone who was a better friend to Michelle than good ol' Steve.

Persistence Is for Suckers

by David Wain

DECEMBER 3 — 11:45 a.m.

In my apartment, on my couch. I take a deep breath, dial Debra's number, and press SEND. RING . . . RING . . . She answers.

>   DEBRA
>   Hello?

>   ME
>   Hey! It's David Wain. I met
>   you the other night at that
>   party?

>   DEBRA
>   Uh-huh?

>   ME
>   You gave me your number, we
>   talked about hanging out this
>   week?

                              DEBRA
               Okay . . .

                                ME
               Remember I sat on the plate
               of cupcakes and had to take
               off my jeans? And we laughed,
               and then we made out?

                              DEBRA
               Oh! Yes! Cupcake Guy! How are
               you?

                                ME
               Good, good. Jeans are washed
               now, so that's over.

      I start flipping channels on my TV while
      talking, hoping it will make my voice sound
      casual, like I don't care too much.

                          ME (CONT'D)
               So do you want to grab a
               drink sometime?

                              DEBRA
               Sure, that'd be fun!

                                ME
               How about tonight?

                              DEBRA
               Perfect! Let me know.

> ME
> I'm letting you know now!
> Let's go to Bar Six tonight
> for a drink, say at eight?

> DEBRA
> Cool! Leave me a message and
> we can figure it out.

> ME
> No need. Just meet me there
> at eight.

> DEBRA
> Great. Keep me posted.

I hang up, slightly confused. But psyched.

DECEMBER 5 — 2:11 p.m.

Walking down the street, casual gait, dialing phone.

> DEBRA
> Hello?

> ME
> Hey, it's David Wain.

> DEBRA
> Hey, you! I thought we were
> gonna have a drink the other
> night.

                    ME
          Yeah, you never showed up!

                    DEBRA
          I never heard from you so I
          figured it wasn't happening.

I do the old "hold the phone in front of my
face and squint at it" bit.

                    ME
          Well, hey . . . tonight I
          have a reservation at Joe's
          Pub for this great jazz show,
          and we can have dinner there
          too.

                    DEBRA
          Wow, that sounds really
          great. I'll get dressed up!

                    ME
          But they'll give up our seats
          if we're not there on time,
          so meet me out front no later
          than 7:45, okay?

                    DEBRA
          I really look forward to
          this, David. See you at Joe's
          Pub at 7:45.

DECEMBER 5 — 7:50 p.m.

Outside Joe's pub. Freezing.

>   ME
> Hi, Debra, it's David. It's
> ten to eight and I'm outside
> Joe's Pub and you're not
> here. I'll try you at home,
> but I hope you're on your
> way.

DECEMBER 5 — 7:52 p.m.

>   ME
> Hey . . . David Wain. I left
> a message on your cell,
> thought I'd try you at home
> just in case. Call me, I'm at
> Joe's Pub. Astor Place and
> Lafayette Street. Call me.

DECEMBER 5 — 8:06 p.m.

>   ME
> Hey, so I'm going in. Tell
> the person at the door you're
> with me and hopefully they'll
> let you in. If you're not
> coming, just let me know.

DECEMBER 6 — 11:19 a.m.

Groggy, in bed, angry, dialing.

>   DEBRA
>   Hello?

>   ME
>   Hey, it's David Wain.

>   DEBRA
>   Hey, you! What's going on?

>   ME
>   Well . . . you were supposed
>   to meet me at Joe's Pub last
>   night.

>   DEBRA
>   I know, I guess we sort of
>   blew each other off, huh?

>   ME
>   I don't know if I'd put it
>   that way.

>   DEBRA
>   Hey, can I call you back in
>   like two minutes? I have to
>   pick up the other line.

>   ME
>   Sure. But do call me back
>   because—

And she's gone. Put sleep mask on, go back to bed. DREAM about horsies.

DECEMBER 9 — 7:03 p.m.

> DEBRA
> Hello?

> ME
> Hey, it's David Wain.

> DEBRA
> What's up?

> ME
> You were supposed to call
> me back the other morning,
> and I've been leaving you
> messages for the last two
> days.

> DEBRA
> Oh shit, I suck, sorry—my
> mom's been in town and I've
> been crazed.

Stand up for yourself, David! Don't let her walk all over you like that!

> ME
> It's a little annoying.

                    DEBRA
          Can I make it up to you? Can
          I take you out to dinner
          tonight?

                    ME
          Sure.

                    DEBRA
          Meet me at Gusto at eight?

                    ME
          Okay.

Check hair in mirror. Thinning, dirty, but
I can make it work for a candlelit dinner
at Gusto.

DECEMBER 10 — 7:03 p.m.

                    DEBRA
          Hello?

                    ME
          Hi, Debra, it's David.

                    DEBRA
          Hey, you. Did you have fun
          last night?

                    ME
          Definitely, though I feel like
          we didn't get a chance to
          really talk, since there were
          sixteen of your other friends
          at the table, and the two of
          us literally didn't talk.

                    DEBRA
          I know—my friends tend to
          dominate the conversation.
          Aren't they so funny?

No. They were not funny.

                    ME
          Yes. They were hilarious. But
          . . . I went to the bathroom
          and then you were all gone.

                    DEBRA
          Yeah, we didn't know where
          you went. We went drinking
          and I tried to call you.

                    ME
          You did?

                    DEBRA
          Yeah, I guess your phone
          wasn't working.

I stare at phone I am currently talking on.
It is working.

DECEMBER 29 — 7:05 p.m.

Debra's lobby. The doorman smiling at me,
me smiling back.

>   DEBRA
> Hello?

>   ME
> Hey . . . I'm in your lobby.

>   DEBRA
> David?

>   ME
> Remember, we're going to
> sushi? We talked about this
> an hour ago?

>   DEBRA
> Would you mind terribly if
> I take a rain check, David?
> My best friend Jeff just got
> dumped and I need to be with
> him right now.

Enough.

>   ME
> Sure. Have a nice life.

> DEBRA
> Don't be like that! I really
> like you and really want to
> see you. I want you to be my
> date for New Year's.

> ME
> Really?

> DEBRA
> Yeah! We can get together
> in the afternoon and get
> dressed, we'll have some
> champagne here, then party
> hop all night. You and me.

> ME
> Okay.

> DEBRA
> Let's make a plan now, so
> neither of us flakes. I'll
> come to your apartment right
> from work. I'll bring a few
> options and we'll have a
> fashion show.

> ME
> Fun!

> DEBRA
> Okay, sweetie. See you then.

DECEMBER 31 — 5:00 p.m.

New Years Eve. Crisp blue shirt is ON.
Ready to par-tay. Call up Deb.

> DEBRA
> Hello?

> ME
> It's me, David.

> DEBRA
> Hey! Can't wait for tonight.
> I might have to stay just a
> few minutes late at work—the
> boss wants to have a New
> Year's toast at the end of
> the day—but I'll be there
> within an hour, okay?

> ME
> Good!

DECEMBER 31 — 6:45 p.m.

> DEBRA
> Hi! Don't kill me! I'm
> literally leaving the office
> right now. I hope you have
> the champagne on ice! Happy
> almost New Year!

                    ME
        No problem! See you in a bit.

I put on the TV. Times Square heating up.

DECEMBER 31 — 7:30 p.m.

Staring at TV. Blood beginning to boil.

                    ME
        Hey? Where are you? I'm at
        home waiting.

DECEMBER 31 — 7:40 p.m.

                    ME
        It's David. Where are you?
        Call me.

DECEMBER 31 — 7:58 p.m.

                    ME
        Okay, I don't know where
        you are. I'm gonna go to my
        friend Marisa's party. But
        I have my cell, so call me.
        Please.

DECEMBER 31 — 9:00 p.m.

At Marisa's sitting on the coats, on the
bed.

> ME
> Hey, I hope you're okay. I'm
> at Marisa's. You have the
> address but I also texted it
> to you . . . along with the
> number for the land line.
> Call me!

DECEMBER 31 — 9:45 p.m.

> ME
> Where the fuck are you?

DECEMBER 31 — 11:00 p.m.

> ME
> Fuck you, Debra.

DECEMBER 31 — 11:59 p.m.

> ME
> Well I don't know where
> you are but it's about ten
> seconds until the New Year,
> and I hope you're having fun.
> 5-4-3-2-1 and hey! Suck my
> cock, bitch! Good-bye.

JANUARY 1 — 2:38 a.m.

Outside on the street. No cabs. So cold I
take a piss and it freezes upon hitting the
street sign.

> DEBRA
> Hello???

> ME
> Hey.

> DEBRA
> David Wain! Hey! David Wain!
> Where have you been all
> night? I've been meaning to
> call you!

She sounds drunk, at least.

> ME
> Have you?

> DEBRA
> I had the most insane night.
> I think I'm on 'shrooms.

> ME
> Where are you now?

> DEBRA
> Walking my dog. Gotta go to
> sleep.

> ME
> You blew me off!

> DEBRA
> No, no . . . I was with
> these amazing people. You
> should have been there. We
> were dancing at this surreal
> party. Call me tomorrow?

JANUARY 9 — 3:00 p.m.

At home. Surfing the net (not porn). Phone
rings.

> ME
> Hello?

> DEBRA
> Hey, it's Debra, I just
> knocked on your door. but
> you're not home.

> ME
> Actually I am home, and I
> heard you knocking. And I saw
> you through the peephole.

> DEBRA
> I came over to apologize for
> New Year's. Will you let me
> in?

                    ME
Sure. Leave me a message and
let me know when you want to
come in.

                    DEBRA
I'm still in your hallway,
just let me in.

                    ME
Cool. Keep me posted, let me
know.

                    DEBRA
Open the door!

                    ME
Text me!

                THE END

Lesson 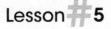5 The Heart Is a Choking Hazard

by Stephen Colbert

Author's note: In the service of this anthology, I was happy to write the following story. However, before I turned it in, I thought it best to hand it over to my wife to make sure I didn't reveal anything too personal, say anything defamatory, or in any way appear to be holding a candle for my former flame. As a result, the story has been mildly redacted, but the heart of it is, I believe, untouched.

When I was living in ███████████ I had a girlfriend named ████. I forget if it had an *e* at the end. I don't think so. I like the name ████ with an *e*. And I ████ her. But when I try to think of how her name was spelled, there is a little disappointed ghost sitting in the place where that *e* would be.

████ and I met just after college waiting tables at ██████████ in ██████████, ██████████. She was small and blonde and very ████████ and laughed at my Elvis Costello jokes.

In a lot of ways she was good to me. She got me to stop playing that game where you █████████████████████████ and stab a ████████████████████████████ as fast as you can, changing the order of ████████████ so you don't get too competent at any one pattern. I guess I owe her one for that. Then again, she may have given me ██████████. The tests were inconclusive.

We dated for three and a half years, the last three of which she didn't really want me to ███████████. I never got a real reason for that. Once she said ████████ to me was like ████████. Another time she said my ████ was too ████. I'd like to think one of those answers was a lie.

After three years, she gave me The Ultimatum: either we get married or we break up. I said, "███████████████████, ███ or do you know some other way to have children?"

███.

When I got back from the trip, ████ was waiting in her apartment with champagne—a ███████ing *split* of champagne, I might add—I guess she didn't want me getting *drunk*. She toasted our time together and then broke up with me.

I ██ ███████████████."

She disagreed and asked me to move my stuff out that night.

Unfortunately, ████ and I worked at the same restaurant. I was a lunch waiter, and she worked the dinner shift as a ███████████. (I think she was ███████ with the head ██████, but that is based completely on hearsay, and I hope ██████ edits that out. But if it *is* true, and that humorless, ████████, ████████, ████████ did ████████ another man or *men* at the same time I was waiting like a monk for her to feel like ████████, it explains a lot. It would certainly explain how she got ████████ when I was on the road half the goddamn year and could count on one hand the number of times we ████████. ████, I could ████████!)

Anyway, as a waiter, my one big meal of the day was after work, and by the time my employee pasta would be ready, she'd waltz in for the night shift, looking ████████ and ████████, and I just wouldn't feel like eating anymore.

I lost fifty pounds in three months.

In those early days after she broke up with me, I would go for a long run every night before bed to try to kill my brain until dawn. One night before my medicinal jog, a friend called to ask if I wanted to meet up for a beer. He was finishing a late shift at a chophouse and suggested we meet at his apartment and go out from there.

Even though I knew that he lived right behind ███'s apartment, I agreed. Maybe ██████████. I'm not sure. But I ran over. (It was a short run. I had moved into her neighborhood after we broke up.)

When I arrived he wasn't home yet. And because there were no chairs on his porch, I sat down on the decking and waited with my back against the door. From that low position, I stared out through the bars of his railing at the dark windows of ███'s apartment just ten yards away, ████████ she would come home soon, and I could ███ her from my hidden perch. Maybe I would ████████ ████████. Maybe not.

Her lights came on. I could see straight into her kitchen as she walked in with a man (I think it was ████████) and lead him by the hand ████████. The lights went off again.

████████ minutes later, the living room lights come on, and she came out of the ████████ wearing only ████████ ████████. She got a glass of water and returned to the ████████, taking a small sip along the way, no doubt to ████████ the ████████ ████████ her ████.

The light went out again. They stayed out for the entire ████████ ████ that I sat there ████████ behind the bars of the balcony, watching the darkened windows.

I've never come close to drowning, but ████████ ████████████████████████████████. ████████████████████████████████ ████████████████████████████████ ████████████████████████████ ████████████████████████████

mesquite smoker

on the floor of her grandfather's cabin

?!!!!!

behind the Roman emperor on a chain.
Instead, I just sat there.
My friend never arrived, and I later learned that he
. Since then, he's become a committed Christian.

I was still in my running shorts, and the night was turning cold, so I finally pulled myself up and walked down
Avenue toward my apartment. Halfway home, I passed a storefront with the neon sign PALMS READ in the window. I walked in and a middle-aged   woman got up from her couch

where she was watching ████████-speaking TV. She led me to a small room down a hall and sat down across from me at a card table. She asked for ████████, and I gave it to her.

She smoothed my fingers out on the table soothingly. After a quick glance at my palm, she looked up and said tentatively, "You are a ████████?" I wasn't, but I didn't want to throw her off her game this early in the prophecy, so I said she was right. She smiled and nodded and soothed my hand again. With more confidence now, she said that she could see that I was ████████ ████████ but that I would soon ████████ and in the years to come ████████.

She was right, on all three counts. I've never forgotten her words, although I've often ████ I could forget ████████ ████████. It's been seventeen years, and I've never ████ ████████ and I don't think I ████ ██.

I'd like to thank my beautiful wife, ████, for editing this remembrance. I'd also like to thank ████ for ████████ me while she did. I have often heard that you never ████████ the people you ████████. I don't know if that's true. I do know that I'll never ████████ that ████████, and that's ████ enough.

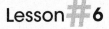# Don't Come on Your Cat

by Neal Pollack

In the summer of 1995, I learned my roommate was leaving town. I decided to get my own apartment, and I needed a companion, which, in those bachelor days, meant a cat. Soon enough, I found one. Gabby was an ordinary-looking gray tabby, though her mother, attacked by a black tom in an alley rape, had apparently been Siamese. After spending a few minutes with her litter, I determined Gabby was by far the most amusing.

My first few years with Gabby were a magical textbook of owner-pet symbiosis. There was always another cat around; for a few months, Gabby shared space with my roommate's cat, Sylvie, a dyspeptic, smelly Siamese who liked no one but her owner and, to everyone's surprise, Gabby. Then I acquired Zimmy, a sorrowful creature with beautiful fur who liked to suck on her own tail. The two of them became close friends. Gabby was never jealous of the women who, on rare occasions, I brought home. She charmed all she surveyed; she was one of those cats who could be called, in that most backhanded of pet compliments, "like a dog." I concluded that she was the perfect pet, that she, in fact, had magical powers.

In 1998, I moved in with Regina, the woman who I eventually married. She had two cats of her own, both extremely needy, enormous alpha males. One of those, Growltigger, was an obese sweetheart with a congenital heart defect. He had the terrible habit of excreting a foul-smelling viscous white liquid from his anal glands whenever he became excited, a process that Regina charmingly called "assing," as in, "Eww. Growltigger just assed in my hair."

Poor Zimmy shrank and metaphorically died in the face of Regina's monsters, but Gabby somehow struck a truce, even curling up in their fat folds on especially cold Chicago days. At the same time, though, Gabby became increasingly attached to me, probably for protection. She developed a habit of draping herself around my shoulders as I wrote at my desk.

One day, Regina said, "Why is Gabby licking your ear?"

"Really?" I said. "I didn't even notice."

"You and that cat," she said. "She's in love with you. It's unnatural."

"Don't be silly," I said. "She's just my wittle pet, aren't you, Gabby wabby?" And we nuzzled, to Regina's disgust.

In the fall of 2000, Regina and I moved to Philadelphia, for reasons I still don't quite understand. The incident I'm about to describe took place in our Philadelphia bedroom, illumined by the full moon shining through our skylight.

I was having a sexy dream, the content of which I don't quite recall. But I do remember feeling very warm and full and murmuring "Ohhhh," if not out loud, then at least in my mind. Then came release, and a gradual satisfied emerging into consciousness.

Mmmm, I thought to myself.

Wait.

What was that between my legs?

No.

Please, no.

I looked under the covers. There, at my crotch, was Gabby. Oh, sweet God, no! I pulled her out. Gabby's fur was completely slathered with my semen.

My brain filled with equal parts disgust, sadness, and panic. Gabby protested grandly as I ripped her out of the bed by her underside to keep her from touching the covers. I held her in front of me at a careful distance, went into the bathroom, put her on the sink, and locked the door.

Out came a washcloth and soap. I turned on the faucet and started scrubbing. Usually, I'm proud of the fact that I'm able to come buckets. But it was making this job much more difficult.

After a few minutes, Regina knocked on the door.

"What are you doing in there?" she said.

Gabby mewed in protest.

"Is Gabby in there with you?"

I was a twelve-year-old caught masturbating.

"Go away!" I said.

"Neal," she said. "Open this door right now."

I could no longer live in my private hell, so I let her in.

"What's going on in here?" she said.

My sobbing began quickly and intensely.

"I . . . I . . . I came on Gabby!"

"You what?"

"She was between my legs, and I had a wet dream!"

Then Regina laughed, not just giggling, either, and not kindly. But it wasn't funny to me. Not at all.

That was the night I became a dog person.

✿　✿　✿

The years drifted by, as years do. We got a Boston terrier, who we named Hercules. He freaked Zimmy out and she started peeing on the couch. Then Regina got pregnant, and we realized poor Zimmy wouldn't be able to handle a baby. We moved to Austin, Texas, and gave her up for adoption to a little girl who, we hope, let her sit on a pillow in the window for the rest of her years.

Gabby got along great with the dog and with the baby. She was still up in my face all the time, wanting to snuggle, to get on my shoulders, to lick my ears. I was more likely to fling her off than not, saying terribly abusive stuff like "Leave me alone, you little bitch." She loved me anyway, and I felt guilty, and also somehow blamed her for instigating the whole mess.

We moved the animals across a thousand miles again, this time to Los Angeles, and Gabby kept on trucking. In fact, she seemed happier than ever. This may have been because we finally, after years of begging on her part, let Gabby go outside. Did it occur to us that we were now living in the second-largest city in the country, and that it might be dangerous to the cat? Apparently not.

One Monday in November, around 6:30 p.m., I went outside to move the car from the street into the driveway. When I was done, I saw a cat lying on her side, on the lawn. I walked closer.

It was Gabby. She wasn't moving.

"Gabby?" I said. Then, I said, louder, "GABBY?"

As I knelt beside the cat, Regina flung open the door.

"What's wrong with Gabby?" she said.

"She's dead," I said.

Regina ran outside and felt for a heartbeat.

"Oh my God, Neal! She *is* dead!"

Our son Elijah, four years old now, ran outside, screaming, "Gabby's dead! Gabby's dead! Oh, no! Gabby's dead!"

We looked at the body. There didn't appear to be any major injuries. A thin trickle of blood had leaked from her mouth, and she'd urinated on the spot where she'd passed.

"No," I said.

At that moment, an extremely tattooed man came walking up our driveway, heading toward the house behind us. I noticed that his earlobes had been elongated. Black discs hung down from both of them. With him was a woman carrying a long-haired little boy. They were going to visit our neighbors.

"How's it going?" he said.

"Not so good," I said. "Our cat just died."

"WHAT?" he said.

He rushed to Gabby's side and felt her.

"Oh, yeah," he said.

He placed a hand on my chest and gazed at me with deep sincerity. It wasn't creepy at all, but because I'm not used to deep sincerity, I thought it was at the time.

"She's a blessing to you," he said, "and she's in a better place now."

"We lost a cat a year ago," said the woman. "We'd just moved to Florida and she was our guiding spirit."

They were weird, but also very kind.

"I had her since 1995," I said. "I've known her, or knew her, longer than my wife."

"Cats are sent here to protect us from evil," he said.

I wanted to reply, "I don't know about that," but I wasn't in the mood to get into a theological argument with a helpful hippie. Instead, Regina said, "I think she was hit by a car."

"She died loving you," said the man.

"No doubt," I said, not wanting to say, "Yeah, and one time I came all over her!"

               ❖   ❖   ❖

The next hour is a bit of a muddle in my memory. Our neighbors behind us provided me with a shovel and a large shoebox. I put Gabby in the box and went into our backyard, where I started digging a hole under the big banana tree. My movements were laconic at best. I was thinking about how Gabby would always drape herself over my shoulders while I was typing, and about how she wasn't going to do that anymore. I also remembered how she shredded my roommate's favorite plant the day I adopted her, setting the stage for many years of naughty behavior. For a while, I had a black plastic stick with a feather on the end. I'd wriggle it in front of Gabby's face, and she'd lunge for it. Then I'd whirl it around in a circle, and she'd lay chase. Then, I'd wriggle it again, just below her chin, and then suddenly whip it up several feet in the air. Gabby would leap high in the air, providing amusement for many years' worth of stoned party-goers. She hadn't done that for years, but she still had a pretty good vertical leap.

From behind me I heard, "Let me help you."

It was the hippie.

"Huh?" I said.

"I'm a professional," he said.

I wanted to say, "What? You're a professional grave digger?" But, again, he was very helpful, so I didn't.

He took the shovel from me and began attacking the ground with a jackhammer motion. His body type (lanky), level of tat-tooedness (high), and general speed of motion (spastic) called to mind Anthony Kiedis of the Red Hot Chili Peppers. He attacked my cat's grave as though he were performing a lunatic encore at the Wiltern.

He handed me the shovel silently. I tried to place Gabby's box into the hole. It didn't quite fit. So I poked the shovel around the edges to create a few extra inches of room. From behind me, I heard, "Hey, Neal, you need a drink?"

"I'm cool," I said.

"You need some bud?"

"Hell, yeah!" I said, and I started to dig faster. Gabby would have wanted me to get stoned at her funeral.

A few minutes later, I scooped the last shovelful of dirt onto my cat's grave, and patted it down. Less than one hour before, she'd been alive. Now she was in a box in my backyard. Life went away that quickly. Man.

The smoke could wait. My family needed me now. Or I needed them. I went into the house where Elijah was watching an episode of *Curious George* on TiVo, sat down beside him on the couch, and immediately broke down sobbing.

Regina rushed me out of the room.

"Get a grip on yourself," she said.

"How can I?" I said. "My kitty is dead!"

"You need to be strong for your son."

"You fucking Protestants and your repressed emotion!"

"This has nothing to do with me being a Protestant. I just don't want you upsetting Elijah."

"Fair enough."

A few minutes on the bed calmed me. Then we switched our focus. We were concerned, at first, that it would be tough to get Elijah through Gabby's death. But he moved quickly through several odd stages of four-year-old grief.

1. Lying in bed at night, listing all the family members who are still alive.
2. Asking what Gabby is doing in heaven. Asking what a soul is when we tell him that only Gabby's soul is in heaven.
3. Asking how Gabby can eat underground.
4. Pronouncing "We have a dead cat!" upon entering the schoolyard the day after Gabby's death.
5. Less than a week later, asking if we can eat "Gabby stew" for dinner.

I think the kid will be fine.

✿   ✿   ✿

As for me, I miss my little Gabby. She was a good companion in the days when I didn't have permanent female company. She saw me through the writing of four books, the editing of another, and the composition of countless newspaper and magazine articles. She moved with me from Chicago to Philadelphia to Austin to Los Angeles. She also left little pools of barf everywhere and consistently tore holes in my clothing with her claws. Basically, she was a cat. But she was a sweet cat, and she was mine, and there's a hole in my life without her, even though I now have to do a little less cleaning.

But I also feel like, in some ways, her death was my fault. They say you cut several years off a cat's life when you let them go outside. So why did I let her, in a congested urban neighborhood? In some ways, I was still trying to make up for how I treated her after the "incident," and to show that I still loved her in the pre-incident way. I now realize, and for some reason didn't realize it then, that pets don't really have memories. They respond to how they're being treated at the moment, and that years of kindness and loyalty can erase a couple of nasty afternoons or weird, semiperverted nights. Yes, you should live every moment like it's your last, and all that, but pets are around for even less time, and we should appreciate them fully before they're gone.

Gabby used to sit on my laptop. Sometimes, I'd leave it open, and she'd sit on the keyboard and really screw things up for me. For eleven years, I made it a habit of running into my office and making sure my laptop was okay. It still occasionally occurs to me that I should check.

But she isn't there.

Lesson #7 Technology Can Be Friend and Foe

"The Internet may not be the best way to meet guys, but it sure is a fantastic way to break up with them."

Eggs Must Be Broken . . .

by Tom Shillue

On Sundays I take the baby out to the park. It is all daddies on cell phones pushing strollers. We look at each other and smile—gosh darn it if we aren't the coolest guys in New York City—in our baseball caps, with a Starbucks in the cup holder. Most of the dads look like Moby. A few look like Wayne Gretzky. But we're all equal in the park.

"Give your wife the morning off?"

"Yep, sure did. Told her to relax, get a pedicure."

"Nice."

I always like to help out with the baby. A car seat has to be adjusted or a whole new larger car seat has to be installed or perhaps the same one has to be turned to face the opposite direction. So I do that.

I help with bath time. Not in a useful sense, but I am there for support, and if my wife has to go get a washcloth, I make sure the baby doesn't drown. I also lean over and make faces so the baby looks straight up while she gets her hair rinsed. That is a big help.

But more importantly I make sure I am always available for date night with my wife. We get a sitter and go out to dinner, just the two of us at a nice restaurant. I'm sure my wife appreciates this—and it's not just because several Web sites have confirmed this is something that should be done—I like doing it, too.

So I'm the perfect husband. And everything is as it should be. But it wasn't always this way. If one pulls back the blinds and peers out into the yard of my past, you'll find the rusting carcasses of many failed relationships, right there, up on blocks. I'm not hiding them—they are out there for everyone to see. But were they really failures? Or did they all have meaning? Serve a higher purpose? Did they all briefly run, and then die, so my current, blissful family life could purr like a . . . I don't know . . . is GTO a car? Whatever car runs really well. That.

To put it in more academic terms, those carcasses/girlfriends couldn't have known it then, but they were a prestigious prep school for Happy Marriage University, where I am currently enrolled. Or rather, each was a prep school that I got kicked out of, before finally being accepted at HMU, which, I'll have you know, was in no way a safety school.

Without a doubt, the two-year relationship, or "fake marriage," is the perfect place to prepare for real marriage. It provides a man all the trappings and pleasures of marriage, but requires no more commitment than that of a softball league or car lease.

Here's how it works: Somewhere early in the two-year relationship, the guy will do something bad. Not bad enough to get dumped, but just bad enough to breach confidence. He will offer an apology of sorts—something along the lines of "Sorry, but that's just the way I am"—which will leave the relationship in a state of limbo. This is the "commitment sweet spot" for a guy. Trust is shattered, but sex continues and the bathroom still smells good.

For those wondering how that breaks down into a formula, it is this:

Happy Fake Marriage→Callous Behavior→Half Apology→Détente

The relationship will slowly play itself out, and eventually end, unremarkably. But don't be fooled—these relationships are far from meaningless. (I had nine of them!) They prepare a man for a successful long-term relationship by providing a "what not to do" template he will be able to follow in the future.

In a fake marriage, you will get away with things a wife would simply not allow. For example—men don't like to plan ahead. Women do. In one of my fake marriages, with Alison, I insisted no plans be made more than forty-eight hours out. I would say, "Honey, where I am in my life right now, I need flexible scheduling."

This annoyed Alison, but I held firm. And it worked. I got just what I wanted—no planning ahead. (Alison eventually dumped me with no warning whatsoever. What could I do, besides nod my head and appreciate her lacerating use of irony?)

Now, with my wife, I know this sort of thing would be unacceptable, so I don't even try it. I have loosened up my "spontaneous living" demands, and it has worked out just fine. I am willing to pencil in appointments, vacations . . . all sorts of things—weeks, and sometimes months, in advance. I do this for her, but it helps me, too. I actually like knowing we will be renting a house on Cape Cod for the last two weeks of August 2011. In fact, I'm very much looking forward to it!

Let me use a more vivid example with a different fake wife, Betsy. I did not call Betsy after she went in for surgery.

Betsy and I were about six months into our two-year relationship when, right on schedule, I firmly committed to the callous behavior as noted in step two of my formula. I was heading to Los Angeles for a while, and after several days I realized I had not yet spoken to my girlfriend. *I wonder how she is doing?* I thought to myself one day. *I'll have to call her . . .*

This was really not out of the ordinary in the midnineties. Some people forget what long-distance communication was like in the early Clinton years. Not everyone had a cell phone, and making a call required some complicated steps: coins, phone cards, a pay phone *not* covered in a mucouslike substance. So, we simply hadn't spoken—for what turned out to be eight days. I would have thought it was a little less than that, but it turns out it was indeed eight.

I picked up the phone and gave her a ring. *What the heck,* I thought, *I will surprise her with my thoughtfulness.*

"Hi, Bets . . . it's me. How ya doing!"

A great deal of silence.

"Betsy, what have you been up to?"

A great deal of silence, then an angry voice from the other side.

"You didn't call me while I was in the hospital!"

Oh, yeah. Wow. That's right. The operation. The eye surgery that Betsy was going in for two days after I arrived in L.A. The eye surgery she had been talking about for months, and that she had asked me to consider canceling my trip over. The eye surgery!

Instead of becoming immediately apologetic, I decided the best course of action was to pretend that eye surgery was not that big of a deal.

"Oh . . . wow . . . yeah . . . yeah . . . the surgery. How'd that go?"

There was a sound of a telephone receiver falling onto a bed, then being dragged slowly across cotton sheets, and then a clumsy knocking on the nightstand, and finally tumbling into place in the hang-up position, and then, more silence. Not quite as dramatic as a good hard click and dial tone, but effective nonetheless.

The future of the relationship was in danger. What should I do? I consulted my guy friends and associates for help. Most were married or in relationships and reacted similarly: "Oh, man, that's bad. It's almost unforgivable."

"Start with flowers every day and apologize every chance that you get. It might not work, but it's worth a try."

"Get on a plane right now. Get back there and make it right."

And on and on. I decided to consult with my friend Bryce, a gay man.

"Oh, you poor guy," he said. "Why is she giving you such a hard time? You forgot!"

Thank you, gay man. You can call gay men all sorts of names and accuse them of being soft and womanly, but they are blessed with a steely reserve that is 100 percent pure male. They have no fear. Why should they? They have never had their male perspective diluted by a woman. The pussy whip has no power over the gay man. He has never had to face it in battle. He is not intimidated—any more than the family of four is intimidated by the medieval mace riveted to the wall next to their booth at Applebee's.

"You forgot!" said Bryce.

I forgot. You're damned right I forgot. That would have to do. I would approach my girlfriend with that excuse: I forgot.

I called Betsy and uttered the phrase. To show good faith, I added a little "I'm sorry . . . but I forgot." And the whole thing was settled. That is how it works in the two-year relationship! And, of course, we were left in the "commitment sweet spot" for the remainder of the two years.

Now, I know the Bryce advice would not work for me today. Gay guy counsel can be invaluable to a man in a two-year relationship, but not to a married man.

Looking back with Betsy, could I have handled things differently? Certainly. But the important thing is that I didn't, so the experience was filed away. I learned it is rarely acceptable to forget about a woman's surgery (even if it is what I would consider, by most reasonable standards, minor surgery). I would not do that again. Now, if I am away, and my wife has to have an operation, I call her before *and after*. I visit. There are cards and flowers. And my marriage is the better for it.

This is what I am thinking as I watch my adorable daughter, adorably eating Cheerios one by one off the table as we sit down to dinner. I open a bottle of Côtes du Rhône for my wife and myself. The scene is ideal. And it's real. I pour, we clink glasses, and silently, I toast. To Betsy. To Alison. To all my fake wives. To all my failed marriages. For they have made me the perfect non-ex-husband I am today.

Women Are Never Too Young to Mess with Your Head

by Larry Wilmore

From the moment you know you're having a girl, you're in love. The months leading up to the birth of a daughter are filled with romantic notions of father-daughter bonding. These were the things I was promised. When I fell in love with my future female offspring, the femme fruit of my loins, I was counting on this relationship. The first sure thing with a woman since breastfeeding I've ever had in my life. Well, things didn't quite work out that way. It's taken nine full years to recover and I'm only now able (through the blessings of counseling and psychotropic drugs) to tell the story. This is my journal of those dark days. The days between the precious little love of my life and me.

July 13, 1998
11:18 p.m.

Eight hours and forty-two minutes. It's so weird knowing the actual date and time your child is going to be born. Angie's doing pretty good [*Larry's wife*] but my lower back is still killing me. The doctor said there's nothing wrong and even suggested I could be having "sympathetic" pains. Great. (I meant that sarcastically.) I paid him six hundred dollars for him to tell me he doesn't know why the fuck my back hurts. Anyhow, I'm excited about tomorrow. I've always wanted a little girl and she's almost here. Wow, I'm starting to get emotional. Just the thought of seeing her makes me feel . . . God, I can't really put it into words.

Somebody told me you fall in love with your kids the second they're born. I think I'm already there. Shit, my back hurts. I hope that's not an omen. What if there's a problem with the delivery or if she comes out with something wrong with her? I can't think like that. Everything's cool. She's going to be healthy, beautiful and healthy. Shit, I wrote healthy twice. I'm going to bed. See you in the morning, Lauren [*Larry's daughter's name*].

July 14, 1998
9:51 p.m.

Wow! What a day! So emotional! Angie's spending the night at the hospital. She'll be home tomorrow. She did great. I was really proud of her. And Lauren. Oh my God, what a beautiful little girl. We are so blessed. It was a little scary at first. They took her out and she had this bizarre frozen expression on her face as if she wasn't quite ready. The doctor spanked her and she didn't do anything. My heart was in my throat. Seriously, my mind went to all the worst possible outcomes imaginable. I thought, *fuck, what if thinking about bad shit happening last night led to some bad shit happening?* I don't even think I was breathing. She spanked her again and again nothing. Her face had no color and I felt all the blood drain out of mine. I looked at her, my eyes welled up, I can't even explain how far down I felt like I was starting to go; and then she just looked at me and let out the biggest scream you could ever imagine. Wow! Tears all around. I cried like a beotch. I mean, it was almost as if she saw me and just couldn't hold it in. The doctor said she had never seen a baby with that kind of lung power. That's my little girl! And every time I held her today, she cried. Whew, I am drained. Hitting the sack. Hey, my back doesn't hurt.

July 18, 1998
1:05 p.m.

Thought I'd sneak an entry during the day, it's so hard to do anything at night. Everybody's exhausted. This is going to sound weird but I actually got my feelings hurt this morning. It seems like Lauren cries whenever I hold her. Angie thinks I'm crazy, but it's true. Every time I pick her up, she screams. What the fuck? I don't want to sound paranoid or overreact but what the fuck? That's all. You know what, I'm overreacting.

July 30, 1998
4:22 a.m.

My daughter hates me. I don't care if she's only a couple of weeks old. She hates me. And I am not OVERREACTING! Tell me if this is overreacting: I go in her room to try to get her back to sleep, cry cry cry cry cry scream cry scream cry cry cry. Angie goes in, picks her up and whimper whimper sob coo. COO! FUCKING COO! What's happening to me? This is insane. I try to tell myself, she's just a baby, it doesn't mean anything, but it seems like she's doing it on purpose. I feel like I've been dumped. I'm in love with my daughter for nine months, she comes out and dumps me. Beautiful. I need a Vegas trip.

August 3, 1998
12:49 a.m.

Maybe it's because I'm black. Seriously, I've run out of reasons. I've changed my deodorant four times. I'm using a different soap, different shampoo, nothing matters. Scream, scream, scream. I hate to play the race card but what else could it be?

August 3, 1998
2:15 a.m.

I forgot, Angie's black too so it can't be that. I don't even like Häagen-Daz and I'm on my second tub. Everybody says she'll grow out of it pretty soon. Grow out of it? My daughter has to grow out of hating my fucking guts? Am I the crazy one here? I don't think so. I am seriously out of control. I gotta get it together. Give it a couple of weeks.

August 15, 1998
9:32 p.m.

Yaaay! Lauren's a month old! The family came over, everybody held her, including her great grandfather, and she smiled and laughed and cooed for everybody . . . EXCEPT ME! Stupid family! They're all like, "It's okay," "Don't let it bother you," "She's just tired," "She's going to be daddy's little girl." Well, she's not. She smiled at me once. She had gas and then threw up all over my Tommy Bahama shirt. And by the way, granddad stinks. She's got no problem with the "old people smell" but a new Tommy Bahama makes her hurl. Jesus Christ, give me a fucking break.

September 10, 1985
8:41 p.m.

I fear my son Ron is a homosexual. I mean, ballet dancer, what the hell is that?

[Editor's note: *an excerpt from* The Reagan Diaries *was inadvertently placed in this piece. We apologize for any inconvenience and/or confusion.*]

October 16, 1998
11:58 p.m.

I was at Baby Gap today, buying some socks for "daddy hater." I'm so pathetic. I see a guy in there with his baby daughter and they're all laughing and smiling and having a good time. I was seething with jealousy. Seething. I've never seethed in my life. I can see why people seethe, though. It's an adrenaline rush. Your whole body's on fire. I'm okay now. I try to tell myself there's no way this can go on forever. But it's been three months. Three months. I don't know if I can last another day. I cry and cuss all the time. I need some fucking Kleenex.

October 31, 1998
10:45 p.m.

Great Halloween. We dressed up Lauren as a little princess, Angie was a beauty queen, I was a soulless void. No costume needed.

November 23, 1998
1:21 a.m.

The whole point of getting a babysitter is to sit with the child because you are unable to be present. Not and I repeat NOT BECAUSE YOUR DEMON CHILD CAN'T STAND YOUR GUTS!!!! This was Angie's first day back in the choir. My job was to sit in church with my daughter. That's all I had to do. But no, we had to get a sixteen-year-old stranger to sit there with me so my daughter doesn't scream and everybody thinks I'm beating her. And to top it off, the little jackal dumps the load of loads in her diaper and who's got to change her? I'm in the church bathroom cleaning what I can only describe as debris you'd scrape off the bottom of a lake in hell; she's screaming, I'm gagging, my wife's singing, and the babysitter had an attitude. I'm done. I don't have anything left. Thursday's Thanksgiving and I have absolutely nothing to be thankful for. Great. I just heard Lauren cry. Well, I'm not going in there. She's just going to cry more when she sees me. Cry your eyes out, see if I care. Cry all night, see how it feels. Wait, that's a different cry than I've heard before. Maybe I should go see what's wrong. What am I saying? I guess I still have feelings for her. I'm a horrible dad. I've just been thinking about myself. She's a baby. My baby. She doesn't know what she's doing. What's wrong with me? Have some patience. I'm going to go check on my little girl.

November 23, 1998
1:29 a.m.

That little bitch. She baited me. She knew I'd be weak. I can't take this anymore. I'm moving out.

December 26, 1998
9:36 p.m.

I'm still stuffed. We had Christmas dinner tonight at my mom's. I actually had a good time. I spent all night with Brendy [*Larry's niece*]. What a sweet little girl. We laughed and played peekaboo and laughed and played more peekaboo. It was great. I have to admit and I know this is going to sound weird—thank God no one but me will ever read this—but I felt like I was cheating. Is that weird? I mean, there's nothing wrong with playing with my niece, but the whole time I felt dirty. I even kept overstressing that she was my niece. Everybody must've thought I was drunk. That's a good idea. I should start drinking.

February 13, 1999
11:09 p.m.

Tomorrow's Valentine's Day and I could care less. Lauren will be seven months old and I don't care. Hey look, she's crawling. Big deal. Oh my God, she's trying to form words. Genius. She's eating solid foods. Don't choke. She loves going to Gymboree. Whoop-de-fucking-doo.

June 1, 1999
10:30 p.m.

Angie and Lauren are in Minnesota visiting her family. Lauren still hates me. She doesn't scream anymore. Now she jumps out of my arms when I try to hold her. That's not embarrassing at all. But it's cool. Got the house to myself. No writing job for me this year. I can't stop being a smart-ass in my interviews. I almost got hired on *Friends* till I mentioned the closest they came to having someone of color on the show was when Ross had a monkey. Did nothing but watch daytime TV today in my underwear. I cannot get enough of *Sally Jesse Raphael*. People are so pathetic on that show, it's great. I'm tired of porn. I should make some more popcorn. Lauren left her blankey. She needs it to fall asleep. It's probably too late to call Minnesota. I'm gonna put on some porn.

July 13, 1999
7:23 p.m.

She'll be a year old tomorrow and she still won't return my calls to her. It's like I don't even exist. I've actually given up. It's weird. I think I'm over it. I don't even think about her that much anymore. Hmmm. Why did I write hmmm? I'll give it one more day.

July 14, 1999
10:57 p.m.

Way back in the recesses of my mind I thought something special would happen today. Yeah, I'm the dad, yeah, I'm supposed to be giving her a gift, but I held out hope that maybe, just maybe, she might give me a gift today. Anything. A smile, a nod, a grin, anything. I foolishly tried picking her up to give her a kiss and she squirmed out of my arms. I thought it didn't matter anymore but I was devastated. I tried to put on a good face but I was crying on the inside. Okay, the outside too. Last week, I took out the old pictures of her ultrasounds. We seemed so happy then. So many plans, so many dreams. Our bond seemed unbreakable in those innocent times. Angie's calling. Talk to you later.

July 14, 1999
11:51 p.m.

Angie called me into Lauren's room. She just said her first word: "Daddy." You gotta be fucking kidding me. Daddy! She treats me like crap for an entire year and her first word is "Daddy"! Who does she think she's talking to? Daddy? I get my heart ripped out of its hole for what seemed like forever and that little . . .

July 14, 1999
11:59 p.m.

She just said it again. You go, girl! That's my baby! I knew she'd come around. I wasn't worried. THAT'S MY GIRL! She is the loveliest little creature on the face of the earth. Fucking said, "Daddy"! High five to myself! Angie was so jealous. She said, "I carried her for nine months, nursed her from my bosom, changed almost all of her dirty diapers, and her first word is 'daddy'?"

She'll get over it. She's just a baby.

# Keep Some Secret Admirers Secret

by Eric Slovin

I love getting invitations in the mail. It's always a thrill to find expensive stationary hiding out amidst the usual bills and junk mail. And I've never tired of seeing my name written in calligraphy on a high-grade envelope. It makes me feel fancy, like a Victorian dandy. But I'm never surprised by these invites. I always see them coming. A friend who I know is getting married sends me an e-mail asking for my home address, and a week later, an envelope comes in the mail. It's nice, but no surprise.

I was surprised once, though. It was great. It came out of nowhere. I took my time and savored the envelope before opening it. My name and address were written by the hand of a real calligraphy artist. Not printed on a computer. That meant genuine personal attention! The return address was Park Avenue. That meant top-shelf liquor! I opened it slowly and read:

> *Your company*
>
> *has been requested*
>
> *at an*
>
> *Eileen Silverman*
>
> *cocktail party.*

Now, for me, that was a real surprise! I can't tell you how flattered I was that Eileen Silverman wanted me to come to her cocktail party so badly she actually hired a professional calligraphist to write my name on an envelope for what must have taken, I don't know, ten solid minutes of serious calligriphization. I really appreciated that. I just had one question: Who the hell was Eileen Silverman?! The name meant nothing to me. I was left with the panic of having completely forgotten a person who liked me enough to hire a tradesman with an antiquated skill to write my name on an expensive envelope. I decided to call the RSVP number immediately.

First, let me be honest. The name Eileen Silverman isn't real. I made it up to protect the actual person. But I think it gives a good sense of the social-demographic and religious affiliation that we're dealing with here. Actually, now that I think about it, Eileen Silverman is a little too strong. I should tone it down a bit. Let's call her . . . Rebecca Schwartz.

A woman picked up the phone.

"Hello," I said, "I'm calling for Rebecca Schwartz."

"I'm Rebecca Schwartz."

"Hi, Rebecca, this is Eric Slovin calling."

"Eric!!!" she screamed. "I'm so glad you called!! I guess you got the invite!"

Shit! Obviously, Rebecca Schwartz was my dear friend, and I had forgotten her completely.

"Rebecca, I'm so sorry, but, uh, could you remind me how we know each other?"

"Know each other?!! We don't know each other!" she squealed with delight.

"We don't?" I asked, relieved. "Then why did you invite me to your party?"

And then she explained it. Rebecca and her girlfriends threw monthly cocktail parties to which they invited only a very exclusive list of high-caliber single men. The only way to be invited to a party was to be handpicked and vetted by the hostess herself. It couldn't be expressed clearly enough how extraordinary a man needed to be to merit invitation. One of Rebecca's friends knew me and felt that I fit the profile.

"But who invited me?" I asked.

This seemed to confuse her.

"What do you mean who invited you? Don't you know?"

"No. I don't know anything about this."

"Well . . . that can only mean one thing," she said, her voice turning mischievous.

"Uhhh . . . yeah?"

"You have a secret admirer!!!"

"I have a what?! Who is she?!"

But no matter how much I pleaded, Rebecca Schwartz refused to tell me. She said she didn't even know, but that she wouldn't tell me even if she did.

"The only way you're gonna to find out is if you come to the party. You have to come!"

Did I, though? Did I really need to put myself in that position? Did I really want to show up alone at some strange cocktail party thrown by a meddlesome yenta wannabe like Rebecca Schwartz? Sure, it was nice that she paid good money to have my name written in calligraphy on a fancy envelope, but I didn't even know her. Besides, if there's one thing I hate, it's Park Avenue cocktail parties—even if there is top-shelf liquor! And who the fuck was this secret admirer?!

But, then again, who the fuck *was* this secret admirer?

I was twenty-eight years old and just out of an extremely long-term relationship that had devoured my twenties. As much as I feared the worst, I'd have been lying if I said I didn't like the idea of having a secret admirer. I liked it a lot. Sure, there was the part of me that was convinced that any girl who admired me, secretly or otherwise, couldn't be all that attractive. But the optimist in me was running wild. Hell, I had a secret admirer! Rebecca Schwartz was right. I had to go.

The party was two weeks away, and the entire time I did nothing but fantasize about her, my secret admirer. The more I tried to temper my expectations, the more dramatic my fantasies became. I consulted all of my friends, but no one knew a thing. Outwardly, I insisted she was going to be a disappointment, but inwardly, I saw supermodels. I saw movie stars. I saw gorgeous physicists in lab coats and glasses. I thought of a girl I once met who, I'm pretty sure, was related to the royal family of Belgium. I think it was Belgium. It could have been the Netherlands. Belgium or the Netherlands. Or Finland. Anyway, we had a nice chat. So, maybe it was her. Maybe it was a previously unknown granddaughter of Ernest Hemingway. I had driven through Idaho once, so that was totally a possibility. In fact, there were literally thousands of beautiful women it could possibly have been. Surely, Rebecca Schwartz was friends with many beautiful women, women who would feel right at home at a cocktail party on Park Avenue to which only extraordinary, high-caliber men like myself were invited.

Finally, the day arrived. I had to decide what to wear. I've never been the cocktail party type, I certainly wasn't at twenty-eight, and I was more than a little intimidated by the uptown address. I knew it was going to be a gathering of young professionals, and I feared that my usual outfit of T-shirt and jeans was going to make me stand out. I began to resent the whole thing. I just wasn't in the mood to dress up to impress a bunch of "high-caliber" yuppies. Then I remembered that I didn't need to impress anybody. I was invited by a secret admirer. She was already impressed! She just wanted me to be myself, God bless her! I put on a black T-shirt, my best jeans, and a pair of brand-new Adidas low-top shell toes (genuine leather). Instead of my normal nylon windbreaker, I pulled out a freshly dry-cleaned 100 percent cotton windbreaker. I checked out my reflection in the mirror and liked what I saw. It was hard not to secretly admire myself, myself.

I headed to Park Avenue.

When I got to the building I told the doorman I was there for the Rebecca Schwartz party. He nodded and directed me to the elevator. Twelfth floor. I was shocked by how nervous I was. It had all seemed like a silly joke up until then. But there I was, in the kind of building my parents' friends live in, riding the elevator, about to walk into a party where I'm going come face-to-face with a girl who has a crush on me, a girl I may or may not be happy to see. Suddenly the "may not" part of that equation seemed very real, and very unappealing. I considered turning back, but then, didn't I owe the Belgian royal family at least the courtesy of showing up?

The elevator opened to the twelfth floor. There was no hallway, just a small landing with doors leading to two apartments. In front of one stood a smiling zaftig woman in her fifties with frosted blond hair.

"May I help you?" she asked.

"Uh, I'm Eric Slovin."

"Oh, hi, Eric," she said, the smile glued to her face, "I'm Rebecca Schwartz."

Actually, now that I'm picturing her there, smiling in the hallway in her smart pantsuit, I'm not so sure the name Rebecca Schwartz was right after all. I think I may have had it better at the beginning. Yeah, she was definitely more of an Eileen Silverman. Or, even a Helen Goldfarb. That's what she was, a Helen Goldfarb.

"Welcome to the party. I guess there's someone in there waiting to see you," said Helen, smiling.

I walked in.

For two weeks I imagined a lot of things, but I never imagined what I had just walked into. The youngest man there was no less than fifty-five. The oldest could easily have been eighty, maybe more. The women ranged in age from about forty-five to sixty. Each one looked like she could be my aunt. What if one actually was my aunt? That would be awkward.

In one corner a Nelson Rockefeller type slyly approached a woman who might have been Bette Midler's sister. In another, a bald man with a fringe of dyed black hair was attempting to chat up a woman who looked exactly like my therapist. Over by the window, a lonely man in a cardigan spread cheese on a cracker. I'm fairly certain he was the father of a college friend.

And then there was me, in my windbreaker and sneakers, looking for my secret admirer.

With the exception of a few clusters of chatting women, it was a scene of perpetual lonely motion. There was very little conversation. Everyone just wandered around, eying each other. This was a meat market for the old and rich. No one said a word to me. I wondered if my youth made them uncomfortable. Maybe they thought I was there to fix the air-conditioning.

I quickly walked through each room, but I knew it was pointless.

After about six minutes I went back to the front door, where Helen Goldfarb was still greeting her guests. She saw me and scrunched her face into a pained smile.

"I think there must have been some kind of mistake," she said.

"Yeah, I think so. Why am I here?"

"I really don't know."

"But what about the exclusivity? What about handpicking every guest to make sure that only extraordinary, high-caliber men are invited?"

She had no response.

"I'm so sorry," she said, the smile finally breaking.

I was sorry, too. My secret admirer was neither the princess of my fantasies nor the troll of my fears. In fact, my secret admirer wasn't anything. She didn't exist. There was nothing left to say. I took the elevator down.

A couple of days later, Helen Goldfarb called. She wanted to apologize. She'd gone back to her books and couldn't figure out why I'd been invited.

"Nothing like this has ever happened before," she insisted.

I told her not to worry about it.

"Well," she said, "let me know if you ever want to come to one of my parties in the future."

She had to be kidding.

"Your friends aren't looking for a guy like me," I said, trying to be polite.

"Who knows? Maybe some of them have a Mrs. Robinson fantasy."

That cracked me up.

"I really don't think your friends go to your parties with a Mrs. Robinson fantasy in mind," I laughed.

"Don't be so sure," she said slyly.

"I'm pretty sure," I insisted.

"Well don't be!" she practically purred.

Was this possible? Was Mrs. Goldfarb trying to seduce me?

"Are, uh, you saying that *you* . . . have a Mrs. Robinson fantasy?" I stammered.

"Maybe I am."

So there it was. I had no secret admirer, but I did have my very own Mrs. Robinson.

I was shocked. Like any healthy twenty-eight-year-old, I had a couple of Mrs. Robinson fantasies stored in the old fantasy Rolodex. I was very open to the idea of afternoon trysts at a discreet hotel with a grown-up woman with grown-up needs. But, again, something just wasn't right. I mean, a Mrs. Robinson fantasy is one thing, but Mrs. Goldfarb was something else entirely. Why couldn't my Mrs. Robinson look a little more like Anne Bancroft and a little less like Mel Brooks?

I let the silence linger for a few moments longer, and then I very politely declined the invitation.

A Grudge
Can Be Art

by Andy Selsberg

Our second or third time in bed together she bit her lip and said she had a confession to make. I tensed up and cupped my nuts protectively to prepare for possible bombshells: crabs, herpes, warts, a psychotic boyfriend, a Nazi grandparent, a nameless rash. But it was none of that. Instead she said, "I'm not really twenty-two. I'm nineteen."

Nineteen! Was I angry? Hell no. I felt like I'd won the *Barely Legal* sweepstakes. I pinched myself, then her, and wondered what I'd done to deserve such good fortune.

This put our span at eleven years—scintillating, but hardly a scandal. It was nothing compared to those chasms bridged regularly in Hollywood, where an actor can be in his forties, dropping the kids off at college, and his dream girl is taking nursery school entrance exams. None of that for me—what this girl and I had was positively wholesome.

Ours wasn't just a novelty act—we got along, bantered well. One waitress even thought we were a stage duo, our jibes were so in sync. There was a picnic in the park, the Guggenheim, a Mets game. She had big red hair and a *Birth of Venus* beauty that was all invitation and tease. She liked to say it was a good thing she wasn't *more* attractive, because then she'd *really* be able to wreak sexual havoc.

That should have been a warning. Also, she was an aspiring actress. Also, she said she wasn't looking for anything serious. Also, she drank a lot. Also, I had to buy her beer—suddenly I was the skeevy older guy who gets booze for the high school crowd. Also, she was into diet pills. Also, she fantasized about plastic surgery. Also, she said she had a problem with dating guys and then banging their best friends. And this is just the evidence that to me speaks well of her.

Did all these pieces add up to a red flag? Try a massive, rippling banner of war. Maybe that's why I didn't see it—too big. Maybe I thought I could beat the system. Maybe I just really liked her. Either way—I was all-in, gung ho.

One night, after a play, she called me from a bar and said she wanted to come over. I met her at the subway, and before we'd walked a block she told me she didn't want any romance. She just wanted me to be a friend. I wish I wish I wish I explained to her that she was just *with* her friends, at that bar, and that I was something different—a friend with a hard-on. I should've said I'm sorry and good-bye and been done with it. Instead, I tried to be that friend. We sat on the swings across from my apartment and discussed her confusion. It got late, and I convinced her to sleep over as a friend. She worried it would be awkward. I wish. Watching the person you want to touch, who doesn't want to touch you, sleep in your bed, in your boxer shorts, is searing. "Awkward" would've been a vacation.

Some nights later she told me she loved me "as a person." Unless you want someone to hate you forever, don't ever tell him you love him "as a person." It's like a consolation prize you don't want that leaves you with an unwieldy tax burden. If you absolutely have to love me *as* something, love me as a walking dildo.

And I didn't even get breakup sex. Isn't breakup sex Article One in the relationship Bill of Rights?

A couple months after she broke up with me—while we were still having fraught, sexless rendezvous—she screwed one of my close friends. She screwed him not once, but on three separate occasions. Then she had a threesome with my roommates. My roommates! A threesome! With! From a distance, I have a sort of reverence for this blitz—it took some set of labia to pull it off. But really, I felt like I'd been smashed in the back with a folding chair, then elbowed in the gut. I worry the nausea will never go away completely. And these are just the things I heard about.

And I didn't hear about it for over a year—one of those years where everybody knew I was a patsy but me. I'd known the friend since college, and once, when we were taking a long walk and having an old-friend talk, he asked if the girl at the center of this gave good blow jobs—when he knew the answer from direct experience! I didn't know it at the time, but here was the humiliating vaporization of our friendship. And I'm flexible—if he'd only gone to first base with her, I would've let it ride. A lot of gay couples don't even think of making out as cheating. But anything in scoring position and beyond is a problem. I miss the guy on occasion, but the image of those two repeatedly fucking each other, while I still wanted her more than anything, blots out all the good memories.

Right after I found out, I ran into her at a bar. She was with her new guy, a pip-squeak. If she'd been toting around a movie star, or some Wall Street stud, I would've at least had the grim solace of being soundly beaten. But this dude was her age. And in acting school. She was slumming it with a peer. And . . . they made out in front of me. A fail-safe display, in case I didn't get it. This was a rout. I got it, I got it.

What was I supposed to do with all this? People rarely say, "You know what you need to do? Carry a grudge. An old-fashioned, dense and righteous *grudge*." Forgiveness and forgetfulness are prescribed so often that we're likely to forget the grudge is even an option. But I didn't feel like I had any other choice. The grudge picked me.

It's not easy. I didn't have any experience with grudges, had no good models to follow, so I had to wing it. A year or so after she broke up with me, the actress crocheted me a scarf. Most likely, she really did love me as a person, or at least felt some vague guilt she wanted to ease. I could've just accepted the scarf, held it to my face while imagining her having sex with my former best friend, and left it in a garbage can—maybe on one of those dark, lonely alleys near Wall Street. That would've been a dignified move, with a nice quiet drama. Then maybe we follow the scarf's adventures after it gets picked up by a lovable hobo. But that wouldn't be true to my grudge. Instead, I took the scarf back to the girl at work. I said it was the only scarf that made me feel colder when I put it on. Zing! I was hoping she would cry and be mad at me. She did! She was! I swear I had a grudgegasm.

The grudge is a way to show you care, a way to stay connected. It would have been an insult to let what we had be downgraded to a mere polite acquaintanceship or even worse, nothing. The grudge required embarrassing, accusatory letters. It required sending blank e-mails. It required every meeting we had to be ambiguous and tense. It meant feeling sick when I saw girls who just looked like her.

I started doing some stand-up comedy, and she said she really wanted to see me get up and tell jokes. I forbade her from watching, as my main reason for doing stand-up was to spite her.

She said she wanted to be able to ring me up and have long, late-night chats about her dating life. I blocked her number.

Who knew a grudge could be so sweet? I would love it if a girl I dumped cared enough to stage a performance based partly on my idiotic moves, and then prohibited me from attending. I even started feeling disheartened by exes who didn't hold grudges against me but should. It's like, don't you care?

The good moments of our relationship—when we were both just aggressively happy to be in each other's company—would add up to fewer than forty-eight hours, and that includes being asleep together. It has what people in the relationship business call a long, spiky tail. Now, I'm the only one lumbering around with this bitch of a tail—I'm sure the other principals have long since sloughed it. This freakish thing is all mine by now. A grudge distorts—it wears a brain-path that you keep going down.

If I could erase the whole thing from my memory, go *Eternal Sunshine of the Spotless Mind*, I would. She even looked like Kate Winslet's character in that movie. My facility with grudge-craft is something about myself I'd rather not know. So I'll allow myself this one grudge, and maybe if I don't work on it it'll just get worn down into something faint and powerless, like graffiti on a park bench.

I do know where I'll see her eventually: on a reality show. She is genetically and socially engineered to tear through one of those setups like an erotic tornado. She'll wire the group together, then detonate every basic interaction. The cameras will find her. She'll make for fantastic television. America will love to hate her, hate to love her. I can see the teasers: on next week's episode, Eternal Sunshine makes a *shocking* confession. It will be disgusting. It will be spectacular. And I'll be retching and cheering louder than anyone.

Lesson #12 I Still Like Jessica

by Rodney Rothman

In 1987, when I was thirteen years old, I dated Jessica. She was the first girl I ever dated. It lasted two weeks. Then she became the first girl to ever dump me. For years afterward I was secretly in love with her. In fact, it never really went away, even during the occasional times I saw her as an adult. In March 2007, using this book as an excuse, I called Jessica up in San Francisco to talk about it. With her permission, I taped the conversation.

JESSICA: Hello?

RODNEY: Jessica . . .

JESSICA: Hey . . .

RODNEY: Okay, cool. Soooooooooo . . . let me start with a basic question. Do you remember going out with me at all?

JESSICA: Uhhh okay, okay . . . [*nervous giggles*].

RODNEY: [*nervous giggles*]

JESSICA: Um . . . like, I am having a vague recollection. . . .

RODNEY: [*giggles*]

JESSICA: But I am not sure . . . if it's . . . I would think we may have gone out . . . before I went . . . before I went out with Jon Nelson.

RODNEY: Come on.

JESSICA: He was your best friend, right?

RODNEY: Yeah. Yes.

JESSICA: I think that might be . . . that's what I am remembering.

RODNEY: So you are remembering that you definitely went out with us.

JESSICA: That's possible.

RODNEY: Me.

JESSICA: Definitely.

RODNEY: Definitely.

JESSICA: I definitely went out with Jon Nelson.

RODNEY: You remember that.

JESSICA: Clearly.

RODNEY: Okay. I guess just tell me what you remember [about us going out]. Do you remember how it started?

JESSICA: All right. Okay . . . Okay, now thinking back . . . the last thing I remember is sleeping over at your house when Samantha and I used to hang out and make cookies and all that.

RODNEY: My twin sister.

JESSICA: And you and Jon were hanging out having a sleepover that same night also, so . . . I remember not being crushed out on either of you guys.

RODNEY: Uh-huh.

JESSICA: I remember that you guys were lurking. [That's] too harsh a word, but . . . [*giggles*] . . . you were around.

RODNEY: Right.

JESSICA: And you know, I think . . . we started talking and maybe I agreed to go out with you . . . and maybe—this is like I am reaching back—that you may have asked me to go out and I said yes but I don't know if we did or not. But I think that was how it was. But I am not sure if I agreed to go out or not. Um, I think I recall like it being like it was for two hours or three hours or one of those things like its going out but it only lasted a couple hours.

RODNEY: I remember [it] being like a couple of weeks.

JESSICA: Oh my God.

RODNEY: Yeah, I remember that I was told I should ask you out and it was around the time of my bar mitzvah. So that would like be December of probably eighth grade, and . . .

so okay . . . so it's [*stammers*] . . . so did you have a crush on me? It doesn't sound like you did at all.

JESSICA: No.

RODNEY: So you don't even . . .

JESSICA: No crush.

RODNEY: So . . . so this may be hard if you don't remember us dating for more than a few hours.

JESSICA: Right.

RODNEY: But why . . . but why if I asked you out, why would you have said yes?

JESSICA: I think . . . because I wasn't quite sure what was going on. And I would just feel bad to say no. Maybe it was the first time being asked, or having a romantic relationship. And not knowing what to do.

RODNEY: Yeah not knowing what to do. I think that was . . . probably the first time I ever asked anyone out. In fact, I am sure it was. It was through other people. It was like, "You know Jessica? If you ask Jessica out she will say yes." And I was, "Okay, then tell her that I'll ask her out." Then it was like, "Jessica says she will go out with you," and then I do . . . have a memory . . . of seeing you in the hallway . . . in junior high school after that . . . and really not knowing how . . .

JESSICA: Uh-huh.

RODNEY: Like I was talking to someone and you tapped me on the shoulder and I turned around and like I didn't know how to talk to you because it was like all of a sudden we were going out but we hadn't actually talked to each other directly about it. I didn't know how to actually act or behave [with a girlfriend]. I didn't necessarily know you that well.

JESSICA: Right.

RODNEY: Ummmm . . . how do you remember me? How do you remember me from maybe before we dated?

JESSICA: Ummmm . . . I think, uh, I don't think there was a *Dungeons and Dragons* yet, 'cause I think a little of *D and D*.

RODNEY: You [think of me] and you remember *D and D*?

JESSICA: Okay, yeah, but even like pre–*D and D* . . . like . . . not playing war games . . . but a lot, like boys scrambling about. And probably [I had a feeling that] Sam's brother had a little crush on me.

RODNEY: Oh really.

JESSICA: Like . . . I guess I thought you had a little crush on me.

RODNEY: Umm, was that because . . .

JESSICA: Because you were . . . what's that word? Furtive. Okay, that sounds weird saying it, but yeah. Kind of like looking over [at me], or sometimes not looking.

RODNEY: Sounds like you were [very aware of what I was doing]. What was that all about?

JESSICA: Oooo, ummmmmmmmmm . . . well . . .

RODNEY: I'm just kidding [*pauses*]. Okay, so, okay, so what do you remember if anything of our actual three-hour relationship? Do you have any memories of that?

JESSICA: [*Pauses*] No [*laughs*].

RODNEY: [*Laughs*] No memories. . . . Since this entire interview is based on you being the first person I ever went out with and dumped me . . . is there a possibility that we never went out at all . . . and the entire thing was some kind of twisted delusion on my part?

JESSICA: On yours.

RODNEY: On my part.

JESSICA: Yeah.

RODNEY: Uhhh, you're saying yes.

JESSICA: Yes. I would say so.

RODNEY: Oh no.

JESSICA: You know if you keep hearing something or being told that this may have been possible, you definitely start believing it [*laughs*]. It's happened with other guys too.

RODNEY: Wow, so you also . . .

JESSICA: [*Laughs*]

RODNEY: If there are other guys who imagine that they were going out with you and they weren't, then I am going to float the possibility that YOU are the deluded one. If that's happening to you a lot—the guys thinking they are going out with you and you think they're not.

JESSICA: Oh, there's absolutely the chance.

RODNEY: Yeah, there's a weird brain situation where you . . . like the part of gray matter that let's you know when you are going out with someone . . . you don't have it.

JESSICA: Well, you know . . . I prefer the case that I'm really narcissistic, but yes, I think this is biological in my brain.

RODNEY: Well, do you remember . . . do you even remember kissing me?

JESSICA: [*Pauses*] Nooooooooo.

RODNEY: You don't remember?

JESSICA: Nope. Did we kiss?

RODNEY: Yeah. Yeah.

JESSICA: Stop.

RODNEY: Yeah.

JESSICA: Where?

RODNEY: For real. I will tell you exactly where because I have thought of this probably fifty thousand times. I was going to say fifty times so that I would not seem weird, but in reality probably somewhere between fifty and fifty thousand. No, but I remember this well. It was while we were going out . . . my definition of going out, not yours.

JESSICA: Yeah . . .

RODNEY: It was in my house and it was in my closet of my bedroom . . . and I was there, my sister was there, and probably Peter Tompkin was there . . .

JESSICA: Oh my God.

RODNEY: And the thing that was weird about it was that Peter was outside, and I had just gotten the Steve Miller Band record and Peter was playing "The Joker" obsessively over and over again the whole time we were in my closet. And whenever I hear that song I . . . that's all I can think of.

JESSICA: Oh my God. Wait, like, Rodney . . . I remember that.

RODNEY: [*Laughs*] Do you?

JESSICA: [*Stammers*] You better not be messing with me because I really do remember that now. You know what's so funny, ummm . . . I want to ask you if the kiss was good? But what's so weird is that I don't remember anything about your room and I don't remember anything about the music, but now that you mention the song . . .

RODNEY: [*Laughs*]

JESSICA: I actually do remember the kiss.

RODNEY: [*Laughs*]

JESSICA: What, you don't believe me?

RODNEY: [*Laughs*] I don't know if I do.

JESSICA: Yeah, I really do remember, and I remember because you had a warm mouth.

RODNEY: I remember [the kiss] being . . . I remember it being kind of a little bit of a mess.

JESSICA: That you were?

RODNEY: Yeah, I'm . . .

JESSICA: Or that I was?

RODNEY: No, I remember it being a little all over the place.

JESSICA: You might be right, but I remember it being warm.

RODNEY: That's nice.

JESSICA: And wet, but very warm, and nice warm.

RODNEY: Well that's good. Well, I am glad [*snickers*] that I could help you dimly remember our kiss.

JESSICA: I recall good feelings.

RODNEY: Do you remember when you dumped me?

JESSICA: Uh-Uhhh.

RODNEY: You called me up. I remember being on my parents' phone in their bedroom. See, I remember this stuff. I don't have a good memory in general, but I do for this stuff.

JESSICA: Uh-huh.

RODNEY: I remember feeling that it was kind of inevitable. Like when you called me up, it was, "Of course she's going to break up with me." Like I wasn't surprised.

JESSICA: Right . . . Well, like through word of mouth it probably got out there beforehand.

RODNEY: Probably so [*laughs*]. Like someone asked me if I minded that you broke up with me.

JESSICA: [*Laughs*]

RODNEY: Ummmm . . . so after that was in December of eighth grade . . . so like five months later we graduated . . . like five or six months later we graduated from junior high school and went to high school, and I remember springtime of eighth grade being kind of a really intense time.

JESSICA: Springtime of eighth grade. Big-time. Totally, me too.

RODNEY: How come?

JESSICA: Ummmm . . . I think like I was getting a handle on what was going on and meeting guys I liked . . . and meeting new friends, like people that I connected more with.

RODNEY: Okay, soooo . . . ummmm . . . so that's kind of how I remember it too. We went out in December . . . the tail end of like a time where we were all pretty clueless. By the time May rolled around, people in our grade were having sex. And I feel like in December they weren't.

JESSICA: Oh, isn't that so strange? 'Cause like when you brought up the subject about kissing, I was like, *what*? Eighth grade? That's all we were doing? I remember definitely everyone was doing third base and stuff.

RODNEY: Exactly. Yeah, people were starting then. I don't remember what I did last week, but I remember the first three people in our grade that went to third base and what order that was in. You know?

JESSICA: Me too.

RODNEY: Soooooo . . . umm . . . like, the other thing I remember is you called me up and said you didn't want to go out anymore and . . . before [we went out], I didn't walk around like with an official crush on you. But once you made that phone call [and dumped me] . . . I had an official crush on you.

JESSICA: Right.

RODNEY: Plus, by the time we got to high school . . . you were a pretty popular girl, and when we went out I would say you weren't as popular.

JESSICA: Yeah . . . I . . . absolutely.

RODNEY: And I remember that [when we went out] I maybe I

had this sense that . . . you know, "Okay, this girl is supercute, it's only a matter of time before this is going to end." I distinctly remember now that during those two weeks we were going out . . . walking through [the junior high] with the really cool guys in our grade and them being like, "Aren't you going out with that girl Jessica?" And I was like, "Yeah." And one of them said, "She's a kind of cute," or whatever they would have said. I remember that I was superpsyched that the cool guys in our school were noticing that I was going out with you . . . but also being aware that, deep down, some giant mechanism was starting to click into place. You know what I mean?

JESSICA: Yes, I do.

RODNEY: And by the time, you know, the spring rolls around and you had starting going out with Leo Perelli, this really cool guy, it was like . . . painful. Inevitable. Like there was this brief window that someone like me, you know . . . had a chance. You know. And then [the window] closed.

JESSICA: Oh my God. So funny.

RODNEY: So what kind of memories do you have after junior high school?

JESSICA: Samantha and I hung out and we were friends, but after [junior high school] we mainly drifted apart and I don't remember seeing her so much in high school. But I remember seeing you throughout high school [because we were in the same alternative school program]. Ummm . . . and I remember seeing you and being very aware of you, which is kind of odd because you would think I would be more aware of your sister, and we were BFF forever when we were younger.

RODNEY: How do you remember? I mean, like . . .

JESSICA: And and and [*stammers*] honestly—and I am being honest because we are doing the interview, so don't be repeating all this information—but honestly, I think, like, I always had a little crush on you, like in high school.

RODNEY: Really.

JESSICA: And, you know, and even after that.

RODNEY: But . . . why would you [*laughs*] . . .

JESSICA: Yeah [*laughs*].

RODNEY: But why would you also . . . that's a hard thing for me to process. It's hard for me to process what you said, so I need to change the subject.

JESSICA: Let me ask you a question. It's off topic.

RODNEY: Okay, that's no problem.

JESSICA: Did you test the recording first?

RODNEY: No. It's blinking red and I tested it before, so I am praying.

JESSICA: Okay, I was just wondering, because I can tell you now that there is *no* chance that I can do this interview again [*giggles*].

RODNEY: [*Laughs*]

JESSICA: No, this is a one-shot deal.

RODNEY: I am sure . . . I understand.

JESSICA: Okay.

RODNEY: Umm, I was gonna . . . How is that true [that you had a crush on me] but yet you don't remember anything about us going out in eighth grade?

JESSICA: Ummmm, let me think. . . . I don't know. You, like . . . even if it's someone you are not looking at in a romantic way. Even if . . . even . . . I don't know . . . even if you should have looked at that person like that . . . Does that make any sense?

RODNEY: Yeah.

JESSICA: Okay, so something like that.

RODNEY: Yeah . . . the reason I remember all this stuff so well is that it made a strong impression on me at the time. You know, it makes an impression when you think about it a lot. I guess . . . ummm . . . you were like my supercrush. You were the first hard-core crush I had, and like the one that . . . like I remember most of my interactions with you. I had a big crush on you throughout high school. Does that surprise you?

JESSICA: No [*laughs*]. It didn't—doesn't surprise me.

RODNEY: Did anyone tell you that?

JESSICA: No.

RODNEY: No one ever told you that?

JESSICA: No.

RODNEY: Because I talked about it a lot. I talked about it all
the time. If you just called up any of my friends and said,
"Who did Rodney Rothman have a big crush on in high
school?," they would say . . .

JESSICA: [*Laughs*] Right. Umm . . . it wasn't that.

RODNEY: I don't think I was the only one. A lot of guys had a
crush on you. Was that something that you are aware of?

JESSICA: Oh my God [*pauses*]. Ummm . . . yeah. I mean . . .
let's say that I am somewhat crushable [*giggles*].

RODNEY: [*Laughs*] That's something you walk around
knowing?

JESSICA: Yeah. If it was about dating boys, that wasn't
something I was too worried about. I like to flirt.

RODNEY: Right right right.

JESSICA: It comes somewhat naturally.

RODNEY: Yeah, I think that's . . . I think that's part of why, you
know . . . like why I like you or why I had a crush on you,
rather than the other five hundred people we were growing
up with, is that . . . yeah, like there was something even
when we were like twelve or thirteen years old. There was
something going on that I didn't fully comprehend, but I
knew it was kind of awesome. Ya know? [*Giggles*] And that

I wanted to be around it. Ya know what I mean? It was like a flirtatiousness or sexiness. Now it seems gross to think of a thirteen-year-old like this, but I guess . . .

JESSICA: [*Laughs*] Yeah.

RODNEY: And then we graduated. I remember seeing you occasionally after high school. I remember lots of painful interactions with you. Because every time I see you I basically go back [to that age] when I met you. It doesn't really matter how old I am. Like I saw you when I was twenty-six, and I felt like a twelve-year-old all night, you know?

[*Long pause*]

JESSICA: That sounds nice [*laughs*].

RODNEY: It's a [*giggles, pauses*] ummm . : . do you remember seeing me since college at all?

JESSICA: Yeah, I remember. I remember you seemed the same, like, you know, I feel like I see you, I don't think that you are that different than when you were twelve.

RODNEY: [*Laughs*]

JESSICA: And that is a compliment.

RODNEY: Well, here's a question. So you were like a really a big part of my life, like growing up for me. But I was clearly not that for you. So who was that for you?

JESSICA: Well . . . a couple of people. But definitely the defining person in growing up was Leo. Absolutely. It was a constant something for us, drawing us back together. But my first one would be [*giggles*] Jon Nelson.

RODNEY: [*Giggles*] Oh no. Okay, rank the following people in terms of who you were most into.

JESSICA: Okay, go for it.

RODNEY: Me, Nick Bogaty, Jon Nelson, Jeff Harris. Let's go with those four.

JESSICA: It would be Jon, you, Jeff, and Frank.

RODNEY: Frank?

JESSICA: Wait. No, no, no wait.

RODNEY: Now I have to worry about Frank? Who's Frank?

JESSICA: Wait, didn't you? You said Frank. I didn't make that up.

RODNEY: I don't know who Frank is. Who's Frank?

JESSICA: Didn't you have a friend Frank?

RODNEY: No [*laughs*].

JESSICA: Oh my God. I swear you said Frank. Okay, who are the people again? Okay, so it's Jon, you, Nick, Jeff.

RODNEY: Oh really?

JESSICA: Yeah.

RODNEY: I feel like you are telling me that because you don't want to hurt my feelings.

JESSICA: [*Pauses*] I would never do that. I . . . no way. I am totally being honest.

RODNEY: [*Pauses*] Ummmmm . . .

JESSICA: I am a terrible liar.

RODNEY: You could be lying now.

JESSICA: I really enjoy telling the truth. You know, there are people you daydream about, uhh, about kissing . . . and there are people you don't daydream about kissing.

RODNEY: Right . . . that makes sense. Ummm . . . so . . . [*laughs, stammers*]

JESSICA: Don't ask me the next question.

RODNEY: Okay, so . . . have you ever been dumped?

JESSICA: Noooooo.

RODNEY: Really.

JESSICA: I have never been dumped.

RODNEY: Really.

JESSICA: I am the first one out if I don't think it's going to work, and my psychic says that the fear of being hurt prevents that from happening. Soooo [*laughs*].

RODNEY: Your psychic says that?

JESSICA: I can't believe I am saying some of this shit. Yeah. That's what she said yesterday. You know when it's not going to work and you are better off bowing out. I am not very persistent, but I like men who are.

RODNEY: I haven't been dumped either.

JESSICA: Reallllly?

RODNEY: Yeah, certainly not since college.

JESSICA: [*Stammers*]. Really?

RODNEY: Don't sound so surprised.

JESSICA: But don't you wonder if all the times [you've dumped] other people . . . somehow it's going to come back one day? Because I am. I am really afraid [*laughs*].

RODNEY: More I worry about, like, maybe my sense of what is working is screwed up and I am pulling the rip cord on good . . . on some things that could work. If I knew how to make them work . . . you know?

JESSICA: Oh yeah . . . yeah. I know that feeling too. Yup. Maybe you would like the number of my psychic?

RODNEY: Yeah, maybe I would.

JESSICA: She may clear up some issues . . . underlying issues that you are not aware of.

RODNEY: She may just tell me the same thing that she told you.

JESSICA: [*Giggles*] She can't tell us the same thing.

RODNEY: Well what about now? Do you have a boyfriend now?

JESSICA: Nope. I just had a breakup about, ummm . . . three weeks ago.

RODNEY: What was that all about?

JESSICA: We dated for about four years on and off. On and off and on and off and finally this. I think we are finally broken up for good. He's a wonderful person and I love him very much.

RODNEY: I also just broke up with someone about three or four weeks ago.

JESSICA: Really. How long were you guys together for?

RODNEY: Not very long . . . about three or four months. It was kind of . . . it was kind of . . . sort of intense for that period. But she was in New York.

JESSICA: She was in New York for all of the time?

RODNEY: She was in Brooklyn, and I met someone in L.A. and was hanging out with them a little . . . like not dating them or anything . . . like just seeing them at parties or getting a drink every now and again, and I was kind of interested . . . and I felt I had to choose between . . .

JESSICA: So then you guys split up then.

RODNEY: Yeah, it was . . . we split up, but it was . . . I don't know. It was not a good scene.

JESSICA: What happened to the girl that was in L.A.?

RODNEY: Well, we hung out a little bit. It was cool. It was also kind of a little weird [*stammers*]. It was just like . . . it was kind of pretty low-key. But [then] I had to go away for a few months for a job.

JESSICA: Do you want to be married?

RODNEY: I do, actually. I am kind of into it.

JESSICA: How much on a scale of one to ten?

RODNEY: [*Laughs*] Ummm, gosh. I don't know, like seven or eight . . . I wanna be, like, in a relationship that is like a good marriage. I don't necessarily need a label, but I wouldn't necessarily be against it. What about you?

JESSICA: I don't need a label either. But, yeah, I am definitely into it. I am at about ten.

RODNEY: Really.

JESSICA: Absolutely. Uh-hmm. But I also really want children. And there's a little more pressure for me to get started.

RODNEY: Right.

JESSICA: Yeah [*stammers*], I am absolutely at a ten. But I have come this far, so I will wait until it's right, you know? But yeah, I am at a ten. [*Pauses*] It's funny revealing so many things in my life [to you].

RODNEY: Do you feel like you're talking to me or just taking to some random . . . ?

JESSICA: I . . . yeah . . . it's weird. Like I feel like I am talking to you, but at the same time . . . I like talking about myself, but I would never talk about myself this much . . . in a row.

RODNEY: This is the longest conversation we have ever had.

JESSICA: By far. I think you are right. I forgot the question.

RODNEY: I am not sure there even was one.

JESSICA: I don't know, but . . . I remember now. No, I feel like I am talking to you. It's comfortable but a little funny at the same time.

RODNEY: Yeah.

JESSICA: When it . . . when we see each other again it will be like, "Was that you on the phone?"

RODNEY: [*Laughs*] This is something I wanted to ask you before, and I forgot. But I want to see if you remember this. Do you remember . . . I don't know . . . like five or six or seven years ago, Ross Venokur used to have these parties after Thanksgiving and people would go over to his house . . . and we would all hang out there? Do you remember this at all?

JESSICA: Yes, I do remember. Not very well.

RODNEY: You came to the party with your sister. We were like twenty-five. I was superpsyched 'cause I still had a crush on you, and . . . I became a twelve-year-old. Then I didn't talk to you like . . . the whole time you were there. I wanted to play it cool. So I didn't talk to you. And then my memory is that you left the party with Peter and a couple of people. Then Peter called me and told me you were upset and crying [because] I didn't talk to you.

JESSICA: I remember this. This is great. I can't believe . . . I remember that . . . yeah, you're right. I remember that. That's true.

RODNEY: What was that all about?

JESSICA: I think that was more that I am definitely a sensitive person. I felt really rejected. Rejected isn't the right word, it's . . . I felt really bad, I guess. It's like someone . . . I felt you understood me, so then [when you didn't talk to me], it made me feel bad. So, yeah, I was really upset.

RODNEY: Yeah, I was really upset when I heard that. I was shocked. Because I think that . . . I think by then I had fully accepted that you just saw me as Samantha's brother and I was surprised and confused that you would have that reaction, and then I remember calling you up and I didn't mention that I heard any of this stuff, but I remember calling you up and I basically asked you out, and . . . I think . . .

JESSICA: Noooooooo . . . uhhhhhh, really?

RODNEY: Yeah, but I think I did it in a really, you know, in a kind of way where if you said no or something . . .

JESSICA: It could be taken either way.

RODNEY: Yeah, exactly. But I definitely asked you to hang out while you were in the city. I think you said yes, and then eventually said you couldn't. Like did you—when you would see me or whatever when I was in my midtwenties— did you still know that I had a crush on you?

JESSICA: Not for sure. Don't you always have crushes on people that you had crushes on?

RODNEY: Crushes can go away, but [*long pause*] you basically look the same. And I think when I was kind of younger I decided I thought you were exactly my idea of a pretty girl. It was impossible for me to see you any other way.

JESSICA: [*Pauses*] I am going to sleep really nice tonight [*giggles*].

RODNEY: Now . . . what if I was in San Fran and I asked you to go get a beer with me? Would you get a beer with me?

JESSICA: Yeah, sure. Absolutely. I mean . . . is that going to get a beer or are you asking me out on a date?

RODNEY: No, I am asking you out on a date.

JESSICA: On a date?

RODNEY: Yeah.

[*Jessica and Rodney laugh.*]

JESSICA: Ummmmm . . . yeah . . . yeah, I would say yeah. Yeah, I would say yes.

RODNEY: All right then, I am going to remember that. When I get back to California.

JESSICA: Okay.

RODNEY: 'Cause you know I go to San Fran all the time . . .

JESSICA: [*Snickers*] No, I didn't know that.

RODNEY: Yeah, all the time. I just constantly go there.

JESSICA: Okay, I think that would be great.

RODNEY: But I am going to stop taping this conversation now.

[*Rodney and Jessica laugh.*]

RODNEY: No, now seriously, I am stopping taping. Reeeeeaaaaaaaddddddy?

[*Sound of fumbling*]

END OF TAPE

Don't Leave Too Much Room for the Holy Spirit

by Tom McCarthy

Dear Liz,

Forgive me for taking twenty-five years to reply to your last letter but I just wasn't ready before this moment. I am now a forty-year-old man. I think we are the same age although I can't actually recall. I was never conscious of age when I was young, there was only big and small. Life was like the dog park in that way.

I am writing to you because last week my parents politely asked me to remove the last of my belongings from their basement. They wanted to repaint the floor. I'm not sure why, the floor seemed fine to me. But I didn't argue. I try not to argue with them now that they are getting up in years for fear that the one time I do some tragedy will befall them and I will never have a chance to make amends. I can't stand the thought of living with regret. I'm fine with guilt. I think guilt is healthy, actually. It keeps me thin. Most people think I have a high metabolism or that I still smoke but my real diet secret is guilt. But regret interferes with my sleep patterns and I just can't have that. Sleep is too important.

So when they made their request I just smiled and said, "Sure thing. I love you, Mom. I love you, Dad." And I walked down the stairs, leaving them both shaking their heads at what a perfect child I turned out to be.

I didn't leave much there. A few milk crates filled with college books, some camping gear I never used, a computerized chess set, and a small lock box that contained some keepsakes from my youth. I opened the box and there, under some fake Confederate money from a field trip to Gettysburg and next to a bottle of Japanese shampoo shaped like a samurai warrior, I found a stack of letters held together by a single rubber band. Those letters were from you. They were sent over the year-and-a-half period after we met at Young Life Summer Camp. The summer camp with a faith-based initiative. Two hours on water skis and one hour discussing how to enjoy Jesus and high school at the same time. It was a Protestant organization and though I was raised Catholic, I still enjoyed it. I was confident in my orthodoxy.

I saw you for the first time on the big field. You were my exact size but perfectly proportioned. I wasn't so fortunate. I had a tiny torso and a rather large head. My arms were short and my legs were long and wire thin. You had black hair and brown eyes and a little pug nose. The moment I saw you I understood you were my type. In fact, I think that was the first time I realized I had a type. And my type happened to be wearing black shiny jogging shorts. I thought they looked liked black satin and that's what I called you before I knew your name. Black Satin. Even my cabinmates started calling you that. "Hey, I saw Black Satin, in a prayer circle by the volleyball courts." I didn't mind them calling you that. They always said it with the proper amount of respect; like the disciples talking about Mary Magdalene.

I thought, for just a moment, that you noticed me during the relay races but I quickly dismissed it. Then later that night I thought you were noticing me at the sing-along but I couldn't be sure. The next morning, I was close to certain you were noticing me on the "hike to the heavens." And then, as I was on my way to "quiet reflection by the lake," I was finally convinced. You were noticing me.

I didn't notice you back. I was too guarded for that. I lived in fear of rejection. Being smaller than everyone else in my class made me feel, well, small.

Then one evening, our cabin counselor, Roger, gave us a pep talk. Roger was prone to giving pep talks before each camp event regardless of whether we needed pep or not. But that night was the big dance and I think Roger sensed the rising tide of panic gripping the cabin. We sat on our bunk beds hoping to get through it quickly but Roger didn't speak. He just stood there and looked at us. Then he started slowly moving around the room and standing in front of each of us individually. He would look us up and down for about ten seconds and then move to the next boy. It was very unnerving. Then he stepped back to the center of the room and said in a quiet, intense voice, "Tonight, I want you all to be confident in who you are because God made us exactly according to his specifications." I pictured my oddly-shaped body laid out on some graph paper in God's studio. I wondered if my buckteeth were part of the plan or just a production error.

"And if we are made according to God's specifications then we are divine. And if we are divine then we are perfect!" Roger pounded a bunk and made Peter Kessler jump. And then he looked directly at me and said, "So you should marshal forth into the dance tonight with the confidence of God's perfection regardless of your size, your shape, or your overbite!"

It was as if God were speaking to me directly through Roger. It was electric. I jumped up and screamed, "Praise Roger!" Roger responded without missing a beat, "Praise God!" And suddenly the room was alive with jumping and praising. It was a pre-dance revival meeting.

I marched into the barn on a holy mission. I was going to notice you back. It didn't matter whether you were noticing me or not. I was going to notice you and I was going to notice you hard.

The barn was packed when we arrived. Haystacks and checkered cloth covered tables lined with punch and cookies were spread around the room. Large groups of girls were already dancing as large groups of boys milled about the perimeter working up the courage to join them. But I didn't have time to be shy. I quickly moved to the center of the dance floor and scanned the room. Most of the girls were taller than me so I climbed onto a stack of hay to get a better vantage point. You were nowhere to be found. My mind was racing with possible scenarios. Perhaps you stayed home to read scripture or paint the clay chalice you made in pottery class. Or worse, perhaps you had already stolen off with another camper who had the good sense to notice you back the first time around.

I jumped down and began to circle the room, dodging bodies left and right. My heart was pounding. "How could I be such a stupid dork!" I said aloud. Then, I saw you. Perched perfectly on a stack of hay, hair held back with a bright red ribbon and your hands clasped in your lap. You looked like a tiny movie star doing a photo spread for Ralph Lauren's Fall Riding Collection. *And you were noticing me!* I was momentarily stunned. My confidence dashed, I stumbled backwards and, slipping on some loose hay, I crashed to the floor. I quickly scrambled to my feet and was met by your warm smile.

That was all the motivation I needed. I planted my two feet firm, lowered my gaze, and I noticed you with all my might. A direct hit. And you reciprocated with perfect poise.

I don't remember actually moving my feet but suddenly we were face-to-face. It seemed too good to be true. Three and half days of yearning were behind us. The connection was palpable and effortless. We played the perfect game. You told me you were from Canada and I asked if you lived in an igloo. You shrieked with laughter. I preened with confidence. My joke about seal meat provoked you to reach out and touch my hand. Contact was made. We were on fire. And I knew at that moment there was a very good chance I would spend the rest of my life with you. It didn't matter that we would have to prolong our engagement a few years so we could legally drink champagne at our wedding. I just figured we would have more time to plan the event. But as soon as our affair ignited, fate intervened again, this time in the form of a Dance Caller.

"Pick your partner and skip to the loo!" And with that the room began to spin. I looked around, rattled by the sudden commotion, and when I looked back you were gone. Swept away in a tide of teenage bodies. I had no choice but to jump into the crush. I had to find you.

The Dance Caller barked out instructions. The room responded. I kept catching glimpses of you through the arms and elbows of others campers. We dosy-doed closer and closer to each other, until we were in the same circle. You were still noticing me and I was noticing you right back. The dosy-ing. The doe-ing. The noticing. It was intoxicating. And then our hands met. A charge shot through my body and I could tell by the arch in your brow you felt it too. We started spinning, faster and faster, our tiny, sweaty hands clutching tight as if our lives depended on it.

The call came to switch partners but we refused. We just kept spinning as if we could make the room disappear through sheer velocity. The Caller directed his charge at us. "Hey, little campers, switch your partners and skip to the loo!" But I wanted nothing to do with "the loo." Wide-eyed and breathless, we kept holding and spinning, staring deep into each other's eyes. The other kids started to back away, sensing something divine was happening, something that transcended the realm of square dancing. A few counselors tried to intervene but we could not be slowed. They simply bounced off us. We were fused, anointed by the Holy Spirit.

The other kids started to chant. "Love Spin. Love Spin." And our speed increased. Finally, one of the counselors climbed onto the stage and grabbed the microphone. He signaled the band to stop playing and when they did he said in a loud voice, "I want you two to separate right now!" But we were joined by God and let no man put us asunder. We increased our speed and now, without the band playing, you could hear the whir of our spin. It was a celestial sound. I imagined it was similar to the sound of angels at play.

"In the name of God, I compel you to let go!" he boomed over the microphone.

How dare he compel us in the name of God. Our Love Spin was clearly an act of God. It was a manifestation of all that is Holy. I shook my head in disbelief and rolled my eyes at the hypocrisy of it all. And that's when I saw the flicker in your eyes. But it couldn't be. It just didn't seem possible. Then you blinked and I knew it was true. Doubt. I tried to lock eyes with you, to reassure you, to convince you, but it was useless. You were corrupted. Your doubt breached our Love Spin and we started to lose velocity. Then I felt your fingers slipping. And I knew, at that moment, the end was inevitable. Finally, you locked eyes with me and simply mouthed the words "I'm sorry." And you let go.

I fell backwards into an abyss of darkness, dumped among the scattered hay. I watched from the floor as you were swept into the air, your tiny legs dangling lifelessly in the arms of a counselor. You surrendered our passion. And then you were gone. And so was our love. Forever.

When camp was over I returned home and I stopped attending Young Life meetings. My friends thought I just lost interest and I never let on. Then, later that summer, I received your first letter. My mother handed it to me with a sly smile and a wink. I tried to play it off like I received letters from women in other countries all the time. I dashed up to my room and ripped it open. I shook as I read it. Your words were so delicate and tender. There was even a cute drawing of you in an igloo eating seal meat. I must have read that letter thirty-five times. And they kept coming every two or three weeks—long, detailed accounts of your life in Quebec, each one ending with a gentle plea for me to reply. But I never did. I never even thought about it. I understood you were trying to reconnect, to fix what you had broken, but it was too late. I couldn't forgive you for letting go.

When your letters finally stopped arriving, I simply put a rubber band around them and locked them in a metal box. I think I put the bottle of samurai shampoo in there to guard them, like an Egyptian burial site, but I can't be sure.

I sat on the basement floor all afternoon reading your letters and drinking Coors Light from my father's private stock. The letters were as funny and touching as they were so many years ago. As night fell I lit some old Christmas candles to make up for the poor lighting. Finally, I arrived at the last letter. I read it slowly, the same way you read the last pages of a great novel hoping it will never end and that's when it happened. That's when I read those twenty words in the last paragraph of your last letter that have forever changed me.

You wrote, "Well, I have to stop writing now. My palm is sweating and that makes it hard to grip the pen. I'm sorry. That's gross."

I gasped and then I took a long pull of my Coors Light. I crushed the can, threw it on the large stack of empties, and then said out loud, "We just never stop learning. Oh no, my friend, we never do." And I read the words again and again.

You never stopped loving me, Liz. You didn't give up on me that night. You didn't let go of my hands. You slipped away due to some physiological disorder, which was probably inherited in the first place. Our love was done in not by your doubt or weakness but by your sweaty palms. That's what you meant when you mouthed "I'm sorry." You were sorry that you had gross sweaty palms!

But my pride, my silly male pride, wouldn't let me see that. No! I was too ready to blame you for betraying me and all that was sacred. And in doing so I condemned myself to a life of mistrust and loneliness. "God, I'm fucking lonely!" I muttered, cracking open another can of Coors Light. "And I have no one to blame but myself."

You see, Liz, sometimes, when we anticipate the worst in people, we destroy what's best. I'm so sorry for not responding to your letters. Your sweet and lovely letters. The loss is as always, mine.

Unless of course, you are still single. Then perhaps we could arrange to meet up and have dinner or at least a drink at some point. I just happen to be single right now myself. I know it's been a long time but maybe it's worth a shot if you are, in fact, still single. I mean if you're married or engaged then just disregard this. Unless you're unhappy in said arrangement and then perhaps we could work something out. I could even come see your igloo. (Ha ha!) So let me know. I look forward to hearing from you. Write back soon!

Warm Regards,

Tom

Lesson #14 I Am a Gay Man

by Dan Savage

Wendy had something special, a certain something very few twenty-one-year-old women have today. Wendy had pubic hair.

Wendy's pubes were the only thing that came to mind after I spent two days wracking my brain trying to think of something nice to say about her vagina. Wendy was good to me. She gave me what she thought I wanted—no, that's not fair. She gave me what I told her I wanted. She gave me what I had spent the previous three years trying to convince myself I wanted.

Pussy.

And how do I pay her back? Two decades later I write an essay about how thoroughly her vagina horrified me. (Please note: I said Wendy's vagina horrified *me*, I didn't say Wendy's vagina was *horrifying*. It's an important distinction, one we'll be discussing further, at length.)

I wanted to open up by saying one nice thing about Wendy's vagina—I didn't want to come across as a gay cad (a gad?)—before I set off on a little stroll down Repressed Memory Lane. So here it is: Wendy's vagina was well concealed. Unlike today's waxed, shaved, defoliated, clear-cut vaginas, Wendy's vagina was discretely hidden under what, by modern standards, could only be described as a Van Gogh haystack of curly brown pubic hair.

Wendy's vagina was nothing like the glistening pink roadkill I'd seen in my older brothers' porn magazines. It was so well concealed, I didn't get a really good look at it. Not that I tried, mind you. Whether I failed to get a good a look at Wendy's vagina because her pubic hair concealed it so completely or because my eyes instinctively shifted from her knees to her navel and back, skipping everything in between, well, that's lost in the mists of time. Whatever the reason, whatever resulted in Wendy's vagina being so well concealed—her pubic hair or my squeamishness—I am forever grateful for it.

A few relevant details about Wendy: She was twenty-one. She was my eldest brother's ex-girlfriend. I lost my virginity to her in a tent, in the middle of the day, in the middle of the summer, in the middle of my fifteenth year. According to the laws of the great state of Illinois, Wendy was guilty of statutory rape. If Wendy were twenty-one and banging fifteen-year-old boys today she could easily do twenty-five years in prison and forever be labeled a "sex offender" when she got out. But back in 1980 the role of sexual initiator was still an honored one. So even when my brother and parents found out—and I made damn sure they all found out—no one thought to call the police. Not even my father.

Did I mention my father was a cop?

Now the details get more sordid: My first time? Sloppy seconds.

Alex, age twenty-three, was Wendy's idea, but I didn't object—not to Alex being there or to Alex going first or to Alex being so fucking hot. Wendy felt Alex should be first because Alex knew what he was doing and I didn't. Alex elbowed me in the side and told me to watch him.

I watched Alex like a dog watches steak.

Then it was my turn. I remember thinking that Wendy's vagina felt nothing like my right hand. It was . . . damper. More humid. And looser—much, much looser.

I humped away at Wendy. Then I started to worry. What if I couldn't keep it up? What if I couldn't come? If I couldn't finish, I feared Alex and Wendy would look at each other, say, "Oh my God, he's gay!" in unison, and then Alex would beat the shit out of me for watching him like a dog watches steak.

I kept humping, humping, humping.

My concentration began to flag, partly deflating my erection, as condensation dripped onto my back from the top of the tent. I think Alex was getting frustrated—it was hot in that tent, and he was ready to split—but he was too gentlemanly a statutory rapist to leave before I finished. So Alex did something that I, at fifteen, figured Alex could do because he was straight. To help me get there, Alex reached between my legs and cupped my balls.

It helped.

I slept with Wendy in part to scandalize my family with my blatant, and unexpected, heterosexual behavior. I made damn sure my mother "overheard" my late-night phone conversations with Wendy, theatrically whispered; I left notes and letters from Wendy laying out for my brothers to "find." I stayed out all night. My family had long suspected I might be gay—asking my parents to take me to the national tour of *A Chorus Line* for my thirteenth birthday didn't help—but my family was Catholic *and* religious. So even though I knew I was gay, and even though everyone else knew, and even though I knew they knew, we also all knew—knowed? —that I was never going to come out.

That meant I had to learn to like pussy. So I had to go out there and find a Wendy, a series of them, women I could fool, women I could take advantage of. And, yes, I was, at fifteen, taking advantage of twenty-one-year-old Wendy.

These were my options: fake being straight or join the priest-hood.

While the big house, fancy dresses, and naïve altar boys were tempting, I had concluded the priesthood wasn't for me. So even though I could never truly fall in love with a woman and even though every fiber of my being screamed "No!" it was my intention to live a straight life. I was going to find a slightly boyish, flat-chested woman, fuck her just enough to fool her, keep her busy with babies, and bang the occasional callboy on the side.

But could I do it? Could I fuck a woman? Could I learn to like pussy? I had to find out before I married one.

The first time I slept with Wendy was a success, it's true, and I was relieved that I could do this thing. I could put my dick in a woman and leave it there until I came. But I also knew that it wasn't enough for me to like pussy when it was full of some hot guy's spunk, or some hot guy was cupping my balls and lying beside me. That set of circumstances seemed unlikely to occur with any frequency in, say, my anticipated heterosexual marriage. No, I had to learn to like how pussy smelled and how it tasted and how it felt all by its lonesome. Or learn how to tolerate it, like so many closeted gay men before me.

Alex wasn't around the second time I slept with Wendy. We were at one of her friends' apartments, just two blocks from my parents' home. This time it was just the two of us. We started making out. Wendy got undressed. I got undressed. And there we were, standing together, in the living room, the two us, bare-ass naked.

I missed Alex.

Wendy guided my hand down.

I missed Alex more.

Today third base is—what? Double penetration? Pegging? Sucking off a she-male in the backseat of your dad's Hummer? In 1980 third base was finger-banging—it was a more innocent time—and I knew what I was supposed to do when Wendy placed my hand over her vagina. I slipped a finger in.

Then two. Then three.

It's hard to describe the sensation, but I'll try: It felt like I'd slipped my hand into a large, lukewarm piece of lasagna that had been stood on its side. Only this lasagna had a pulse.

And hair, this lasagna was covered in hair.

I kept my fingers in Wendy's vagina long enough, I hoped, to give her the impression that I liked hairy lasagna as much as the next guy. Then I executed what I, at age fifteen, thought was an exceedingly smooth move. I removed my fingers from Wendy's vagina and pulled her into an embrace. I brought my hand up her back slowly. I caressed her—but just with the palm of my hand and my thumb and pinky, the fingers that hadn't been in Wendy's vagina. I brought my hand up to her shoulder. I leaned way in to kiss her neck, positioning my nose so it was angled over her shoulder. I brought my wet index, ring, and middle fingers up to my nose.

You see, back in the tent I hadn't really got a chance to smell Wendy. By the time I got in there, Wendy already smelled like Alex's sweat and spunk. Not that I'm complaining, but the whole point of my adventures with Wendy was, well, learning to like pussy.

Wendy's vagina smelled awful. Really awful. Like no hairy lasagna I'd ever eaten.

I need to take a time out here.

For the record, I really don't mean to be ungracious about Wendy or her vagina. I want to make it clear that I'm not stating Wendy's vagina smelled awful. Although that is, um, precisely what I just stated. Hey, maybe Wendy's vagina smelled bad— maybe she had a yeast infection or something—but it seems likelier that the problem wasn't the vagina itself but the person smelling it, aka the vagina-smeller.

We know more about sexual orientation today than we did in 1980. For instance, no one knew way, way back in 1980 that gay men's brains respond to male sweat, scents, and pheromones the same way straight women's brains do; nor did we know that gay men's brains respond negatively to female scents, pheromones, and sweat, the same way straight women's brains do. Researchers in Sweden added that interesting new item to the ever-growing mountain of evidence that homosexuality is genetic, not chosen.

Okay, let's get back to the hairy lasagna. . . .

After quickly pulling my fingers away from my nose I began to caress Wendy's back again. But this time I used all my fingers. I was pretending that I was passionately caressing her when I was, in fact, vigorously wiping her juices off my fingers. I thought this sequence of moves—strip, finger-bang, caress, position nose, bring fingers to nose, smell fingers, wipe fingers while pretending to caress—was pretty slick.

"Did you just wipe your hand on me?"

"No," I lied. And then we had sex. No sloppy seconds for me this time. Tidy firsts. And I could do it. I didn't need Alex there, my balls in his hand. I could do this thing; I could have sex with women. I could pass.

We fucked around a dozen or so more times. Summer turned into fall, fall into winter. Wendy soon noticed that, despite her coaching, my sexual repertoire was shrinking, not growing. I ignored her breasts, I kept my fingers out of her vagina, my mouth never ventured south of her collarbones. Then one day Wendy called with two important pieces of news. First, it was over. Second, she had missed her period.

I spent a week flipping out about the injustice of it all. How could I have gotten her pregnant? Didn't shutting my eyes and pretending that Wendy's vagina was the ass of this boy I was in love with offer any protection at all? Why didn't my gay sperm, realizing where they had been deposited, turn tail and start swimming in the opposite direction of her eggs?

I didn't have to stress for long. The next day Wendy called to tell me she got her period. She also wanted to let me know she was seeing another guy now, someone her own age.

"It was fun," she said, comforting me. "I like you. You'll meet another girl."

God, I hope that never happens, I thought to myself, listening as Wendy let me down easy. *It wasn't fun. I can't like you or any girl the way I'm supposed to. I thought I could do this, I thought I could fake it. I thought I could pass. But I can't, I don't want to, it's not fair. My heart isn't in it.*

A month later I had sex with a guy for the first time. In his apartment, in the middle of the night, in the middle of my sixteenth year. Jeff was twenty-one, with shaggy brown hair and big blue eyes. I guess he's just another of the statutory rapists I have known and loved. Jeff smelled great. He tasted great. And no one needed to cup my balls.

Nine Years Is the *Exact* Right Amount of Time to Be in a Bad Relationship

by Bob Odenkirk

This is a transcript taken from a recent Bob Odenkirk Rocky RelationShip Seminar.

Hey. How are you doing, couples? Are you all ready to hear about my plan for you to get the most from your rocky relationship? I see one man over there who isn't nodding. Sir? Oh, you're a lesbian? Oh, I thought you were a man [*really awkward laughs*]. You're here with her? Oh, I thought she was a man, too. I thought you were a gay couple. No, I understand you are gay, just . . . well, okay, let's keep moving on.

As I've promised in my brochures, I speak from experience. Everything I am about to share with you is based on real-life experimentation. My theory has been tested in the lab called "My Past" by a doctor named "Me."

Is there a time limit for relationships? How long do you "hang in there"? What's a good "rule of thumb" for exploring every avenue before breaking it off and moving on?

The answer is simple. Nine years.

Now, I see a lot of heads not nodding at that. Probably you're thinking nine years is overdoing it, especially if you broke up for the first time at one and half years and then broke up again at five years and then, even though you were living in different cities thousands of miles apart, you somehow forced yourselves

together again for another four years of difficult unpleasantness. Many people would say three years of general unease is enough, that it's time to "move on." No. You're wrong. You're wrong and you're pathetic. Nine years, you bitches. Nine fucking years. Who's laughing in the back? That was a cough? I fucking hope so, because goddamnit I am speaking from some hard-won experience here and you'd better respect that shit.

Here, my friends, is the only path to a "healthy breakup." Though before I proceed, I would like to remind everyone that this seminar is 100 percent nonrefundable.

Year 1

This is the year of "The Crush." Excitement, energy, warmth, and hope infuse every aspect of the relationship, making the possibilities seem limitless, rosy, and un-put-downable. Not much to say beyond that.

Year 2

Some afterglow remains. You begin to perceive shortcomings in your partner's psyche, which will severely limit your ability to grow as a couple. You get pissed. You argue. Roses make things better. You start to notice how good food tastes, how interesting books are, how marvelously distracting distractions can be. Men might rediscover masturbation and think, "Hey, I'm a pretty good masturbator!" Your relationship is tumultuous, but in a classic pop song sense—this is pretty fun, actually, you sort of feel like a tortured artist, except you're not creating art. Nor will you.

Year 3

Your friends tell you to get out. Her friends tell her to get out. You relearn each other's emotional limitations and psychological shortcomings on a daily basis. An hourly basis. You consider therapy. This is good. This is the beginning of a choice growing inside of you. But you are still five years away from therapy! So slow down! The drama of the relationship is tarnishing, which makes you suspect that it is not actually made of gold, but brass. Here is what you will find out: It's not even brass. Your relationship is made of mold, what you are seeing as tarnish is actually just more mold breaking down and feeding on itself. Fuckin' mold, dude [*uncomfortable coughs from the back of the room*].

Year 4

A pretty good year. Some ups and downs in the relationship. Mostly downs, though. Even the ups are a bit downish. You are using this year to see if you can make your partner's shortcomings work to your advantage. Good for you. You will fail. People around you are "clamming up." They tolerate your relationship like they tolerate the clanking sound in a car engine. After a while it's just there, no reason to acknowledge it. You go on a trip with friends, without your partner. You have a real good time.

Year 5

Your mother tells you to get out. You begin to consider divorce, but then realize you aren't married yet. You think, well, maybe we should get married and with that commitment we can finally relax and let go of the "fantasy" of a happy relationship but find happiness in reality and a promise of undying okayness. And if that doesn't work, then the divorce thingy is a legit option. You are also entering into the arena of long-term relationshippery. You are sort of proud of this—good, go with that, you're going to need every bit of momentum you can get to make it through FOUR MORE FUCKING YEARS.

Year 6

You are going strong, avoiding each other, not asking too much from the relationship. Many of you might think this is the time to move into therapy, to actually confront the many issues that make day-to-day life unpleasant and long-term plans unthinkable. Too soon! This bad relationship needs to run its course, and it is a marathon. If therapy tells you to leave now you will be prematurely abandoning the race—in its final push to the finish. Plan a long holiday. It will not be enjoyable. Attend a wedding for friends who met only two years ago. Look at them and wonder. You and your partner are now in sync, sharing a low-grade depression which swarms around you like hundreds of depressed bees. This is a good year to discover the artwork of Edward Hopper. There's something about his clean lines and composition that will speak to you.

Year 7

Same as year four. Three hundred sixty-five days, not that long as it turns out.

Year 8

Just doin' time. You're almost there. The couple who married a year and half ago after only being together for two years before that—they get divorced and don't seem too distraught over it. By the end of the year they will both be in new relationships. Wow. That's tragic. I guess some people are shallow. They have shallow relationships that start fast and end fast because they just aren't that deep. They aren't as deep as you, you tell yourself, at first confidently, and then, less so.

Year 9

The watershed. You can go to therapy now. Together and apart. You can do all those things you've been dreaming of: crying and collapsing on the floor, crying on the phone, crying in a restaurant. You can finally say, in public, "I think this has to end," and watch the unstartled faces of your bored friends as they try to care. Give your friends multiple chances to care. They will need them. Start to separate your nine years of memories, furniture, and collections and realize it's not that hard to do. It's fairly easy to acquire the *Seinfeld* box set and an Irish knit sweater you both wore. As it turns out, the Irish can't stop knitting. Spend that first night alone. The ghost of your ex wanders the halls. Don't give it any credence because ghosts aren't real. Not like vampires, which are *very* real, but not relevant to this particular discussion. I've said too much.

[*Long pause, more coughing from the back, the sound of a few people getting up and filing out*]

Great. You see that plan? You see how complete it is? How it covers every base? Here's the great thing about the plan: It leaves you squarely sure that you will never enact this plan again. You will have a level of certainty in your life few people ever achieve. You will also have a high horse to ride as you comment on other people's short-lived traumas. Oh how many times you will win the argument when you say, "Hey! Try hangin' in there for nine years!" Nice. You can rest assured you tried everything, including depression and deep boredom, two flavors which must be sampled if you want to feel you truly lived. Why the hell do you think people climb Everest? Because it sucks BIG TIME! They did it anyway, and now they can rub that in other people's faces for the rest of their lives. You wimps.

[*Light applause*]

A Dog Is No Reason to Stay Together

by Damian Kulash, Jr.

Amanda was my best friend's girl. Or at least *he* thought so. They'd had a brief fling eight months prior, and Adam's M.O. at the time was to convince himself he was deeply romantically linked—like right on the brink of marriage—with whomever he'd last got it on with, regardless of how much alcohol had been involved in getting to the get-on, or how much time had passed since it'd been got. Every so often he'd run into his soul mate at a party and she'd have to ask for his name again, which made for awkward moments. Adam was my roommate, and I hated seeing him brokenhearted all the time, but Amanda was foxy, and since a guy is only obligated to respect another guy's boundaries when they aren't imaginary, I figured I was on stable ethical ground when Amanda and I made out after that fateful night at the monster truck rally.

We were a great couple. We dressed funny and made art and took road trips and got drunk a lot. We moved to Chicago together and filled a loft with armloads of amusements from the science surplus store, and we invited our friends over to drink wine with us and laugh at religious people on TV. It was love—love like you see in movies. Except in movies, relationships don't change, or grow, or slowly fall apart. They either last forever or end mercifully fast with a thrown plate and a jump cut. At least in the movies I watch. I suppose Hugh Grant fans could argue there's a whole genre of film built on themes like "Now I Can Truly Love You Because This Maladjusted Boy Has Cured Me of My Selfishness," or "All I Wanted Was for You to Say You Were Proud of Me and My Equestrian Accomplishments." But the movies I watch and the books I read and the music videos I'm not in are all soft lenses and hot sweet love until something suddenly brings it to an end, like, say, the Terminator strolls in and impales the male lead.

In reality, relationships only end this cleanly when one of the participants is a prostitute. The rest linger and fade and slowly deteriorate, regardless of how simple and exciting they seemed at the start. For Amanda and me, this deterioration came labeled "growth." We ignored our misgivings about the cooling fires, convinced that this was what it meant to mature; our needy childish desires were mellowing into something deeper and more sustainable, the kind of love they had in the Middle Ages when everyone wrote poetry, not just East Coast nerdlingers. We were becoming adults, we told ourselves. So what if sex was less frequent than trips to the Home Depot? Adults have significant hardware needs, and if the intrigue of our early days was fading, we consoled ourselves that we were discovering the *real* virtue under there: teamwork. As if companionship, when you boil it down, is essentially a sport, and not one of those coed naked ones from the T-shirts of our youth.

To be fair, it's a pretty pleasant phase of a relationship. Teamwork is satisfying. Sure, on the passion/adrenaline scale, you just can't top frantic sex on the hood of your beat-up Camry, but there is a distinct satisfaction in dropping off her movies at Blockbuster or remembering to use only the approved utensils on the nonstick cookware; these are things that scream *WE'RE IN THIS TOGETHER!* It's a nice feeling, togetherness, and looking back, those couple years were like the warm fuzzy version of a climactic *A-Team* montage; we cobbled together a life

the way Murdock and Face made fully armed tanks from kin-
dling, telephone wire, and two or three riding lawnmowers. We
talked our way into private parties and produce-market dis-
counts, we convinced our landlord to spring for a dishwasher, we
encouraged our single friends to date each other, we shared
winter hats and sunglasses. And, crucially, we got a dog.

Let me just get this out of the way right now: we're not like
those sick fucks who have babies just to save their relationship.
Under the surface, the excitement of the early days might have
been waning, but we were doing our best to ignore the ebb, and
in any case, Ella The Dog was not some Band-Aid or stopgap to
keep the home fires burning. She was a helpless, six-week-old,
burrito-sized, tailless puppy who'd been rescued from a cruel
dog-fighting ring, and she needed a home. But all the same, I
can't say she didn't help out on the relationship front. She
brought us together and turned us into a little family. I loved the
dog, Amanda loved the dog, we all loved each other, and for a
while there, that's all anybody needed.

We potty-trained her and took her to obedience classes. She
fell over when she tried to wag the tail that didn't exist. We taught
her to swim and catch Frisbees and jump through hula hoops
held head-high. She learned to recognize the word "squirrel,"
and just by saying it we could incite Björk-like howling and
vicious attacks on innocent trees. We bought her a toy piano,
which she'd bang on like a palsied Elton John when we told her
to "rock out." When I went into the studio to make my band's
first album, Ella The Dog played on the recording, and she'd lie
for hours on the base of my mic stand while I sang.

You'll notice this is the first time I mention being in a band.
Up to this point my band had mostly been irrelevant to my relationship; everyone has a day job and a pipe dream, and if I was
dumb enough to nurse a rock and roll fantasy, I was also smart
enough not to expect it to come true. But about a year after we
got Ella The Dog, the band reached a turning point and the pipe

dream became real. When I quit my job to start touring, Amanda couldn't have been more supportive; all we wanted for each other was happiness, and happiness, I was pretty sure, meant living on truck stop food and spending twelve hours a day in an un-air-conditioned 1986 Dodge conversion van, elbow-to-elbow with three other sweaty fools who share the delusion.

The constant touring caused another shift in my relationship. Amanda and I went from real teammates to imaginary ones. She was sleeping in our bed and going to her job and feeding our dog, and I was sleeping on strangers' floors and getting paid in beer tickets. While the folks around me, unburdened by monogamy, were engaging in what is generally expected of rock musicians—stumbling from city to city blotting out the previous night's memory with a new girl and a dozen more Pabsts—I prided myself on pining. I had emotional ballast in the maelstrom, a home team to believe in, a woman and a dog to miss. For months on end, our lives only intersected for the few exhausted minutes of our nightly phone call—it was about as exciting, and only slightly less sexual, than a romance between hospice patients—but still we soldiered on, loyal and determined and dedicated. We lasted this way for nearly two years.

But one day I came home to Chicago after an especially long string of shows, and it all came crashing down. Ella The Dog and I were throwing tennis balls and terrorizing ducks in Humboldt Park—which has surely become a thousand-acre lot for some palatial Starbucks by now, but was still knee-deep in immigrants and corpses at the time—when I realized that Ella was more important to me than Amanda. They had both come to stand for the same things: duty and loyalty and warmth and support, but to experience them with the dog was tangible; it required contact. It meant being there with her, and I loved it. I loved the sticks and Frisbees and contempt for animals smaller than herself. I loved the howling and hula hoop jumping and the careful inspection of particularly impressive stacks of feces. By contrast,

Amanda and I had ripened our relationship past recognition, from practice to theory, until it had morphed into a purely symbolic belief in each other, something we didn't even need real contact to sustain. We had lost whatever it is that differentiates romantic love from friendship and now we were just best friends doing our daily telephone checkup. The life we'd built was still there in our apartment two blocks away, but I was no longer a part of it, and all that really made Chicago home now was Ella The Dog. She had become my best friend's girl, and I loved her, but this time I couldn't steal her away.

In the end it was Amanda who dumped me, both of us lying faceup in the bed in the middle of the night, talking the way we did on the phone, not looking at each other. It was pretty low-drama; by then there wasn't much to give up except the idea that there was something to give up. That, and of course, the dog. With a hint of determination that suggested she thought I might argue, Amanda asserted that she was keeping Ella, but it was a custody battle I'd already lost, and I knew it. It stung—badly—but there's just no way around it: you can't stay with someone just because of a dog, and you can't try to take the dog when she's been the one caring for it. (Unless you're a total dick. Then you can do pretty much anything.)

So I just lay there and let it all go; the last traces of teamwork finally fizzled out. The saddest thing, that night, wasn't the loss, it was the thought that there would someday be others: other dogs, other boyfriends, other girlfriends; that all of our diligent future-building would inevitably be undone by real people in the real future. We all want to believe that the people who dump us will regret it someday, but I knew it wasn't true; it was over, and I would be replaced.

And I was right. Now, five years later, Amanda and Ella The Dog live on a tropical island with a gentle Viking who's apparently both champion skydiver and master carpenter. I haven't met him, but by all accounts he's talented at pretty much everything and a wellspring of kindness—one of those people put on earth to teach the rest of us humility. Amanda sends photos of them repairing the moat around their house and rowing at sunset in a canoe he built by hand, and I am—I'm not lying—genuinely happy for them. It's a little weird to see your ex in love with someone else (and maybe weirder to think she could have a kid with the letter ø in its name), but I take comfort that it took a veritable Norse god to fill my shoes. And of course time heals an awful lot, so after half a decade, I really have moved on. At least when it comes to Amanda.

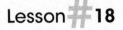# You Too Will Get Crushed

by Ben Karlin

We didn't meet cute. She was taking baths on the downlow with a friend of mine while her boyfriend pined away in Ignoramusland, aka Houston. It's not polite to name names. Hers was Jill.

We took up, falling fast and hard in the waning light of life in a college town after you're done with college. You know, the time when you're supposed to have left already but just can't surrender two-hundred-dollar-a-month rent and the idea that these were, are, will be the best days of your life. They weren't, aren't, and won't be. But it's awesome to think so.

Let me tell you a little about her—for me though, not for you—in order to reclaim that which has been smothered beneath a calloused heart. She had flaxen hair, wispy and cut short around her opal face. She was fair and thin—not scrawny, taut. She had cheeks that shot into perfect circles every time she smiled slyly, which was quite a lot. She was a troublemaker. She made me feel like I was a troublemaker, too. I was not a troublemaker. I am a wimp who still doesn't know exactly what spark plugs do.

We moved through the early stages of our relationship in paces that seem stunningly familiar now—but at the time felt like a fever dream. We lingered outside each other's front doors not wanting nights to end. Walked hand in hand through the farmers' market, envious of no one, living in the goddamn now.

We held out, carnally speaking, partially out of the now comically puritanical notion that it would be better if we waited. (The other *part* had to do with the fact that she had technically not broken it off with Clueless T. McCuckhold down in Texas.) The whole time, one question slowly built in my mind: What if this is the person I never run out of falling in love with?

Alas, like poorly fenced-in pit bulls raised by angry Mexican youths, the complications of life can only be kept at bay for so long. Eventually, they will attack and tear you apart, and unless there is some passerby to pull you out of their vicelike jaws, you will be grievously injured, if not killed. Come to think of it, most of that last sentence is just about pit bulls.

The point, however, is that upon leaving our college town— I'll call it Eden to protect its identity from future pilgrims who may flock there to trace the origin of this very story—mistakes were made. Some were mistakes of vanity. Others of youth. Still others of the vanity of youth. Eventually, these mistakes would pile up and their weight would become too much for any one man, or relationship, to bear. Here are those mistakes.

Mistake #1

I told her I was moving cross-country—to Los Angeles—and wanted to stay together but didn't want a long-distance relationship. Instead of inventing a new form of relationship, I simply moved without discussing it further. One clue this might not be the most mature tack: at least once during this period, we had sex where weeping was involved. "What, are you sad? Did it hurt? I thought it was quite good!"

Mistake #2

Expressing indignation, rage, and heretofore unseen emotions when I discovered she had started seeing someone else in my absence—even though I gamely, albeit futilely, attempted to penetrate Southern California's hyper-Darwinian mating scene. Yes, by my own design I left things impossibly murky and vague—but that was for *my* benefit. Not hers! She was supposed to be pining for me. Hoping that I came around.

Mistake #3

I came around.

On a last-minute, half-baked romantic whim, I flew from Los Angeles to her parents' home in Iowa, where she was visiting. This was a surprise move, confusing everybody, especially the parents, since they knew she was doing some other dude. I didn't know that. Yet.

Why did I fly to Iowa? What was it that kept me coming back when Reason and Practicality were screaming, "Let it go, dickwad!" (You should know that Reason and Practicality are mean.) Well, though the heady days of falling and falling and falling in love were shrinking in a rearview mirror, there was still hope. That niggling itch that if you keep at it, persevere, it will come back. Maybe not permanently, but in waves big enough and frequent enough to make everything else worth it. I wasn't ready to give up. And what came of it?

For a few days we enjoyed something resembling romantic bliss. But, as I soon learned, it would be the roller-coaster style. The kind that makes you puke. I helped her move—not to L.A., where I lived, but to Chicago. On the drive, we went into further detail about each other's sexual exploits during our time away from each other. My part was easy. Zero sexual exploits. "And you? What's that? More baths?" What is it with her and bathing with dudes? Now I got really angry. And sad. I was probably more angry than sad, but I found sadness seemed to affect her more. So I went with that. In a dramatic flourish bordering on the baroque, I demanded to be dropped off—not in Chicago, but twenty miles outside the city at O'Hare Airport, where I told her I would pay any amount of money to escape this nightmare. (This was not true. In my mind I had decided I would spend no more than six hundred dollars for a ticket.)

Mistake #4

I stayed.

Finished the drive. We arrived at her new place and I went right down the street to a bar on the corner. Drank two shots of Jameson, which seemed like the appropriate thing to do. I was in uncharted territory here. Maybe it should have been Jack Daniel's. You know what, I just realized it should have been Jack Daniel's. I walked back, and—at this point I am really taking my cue more from popular music and seventy-five years of American cinema than anything resembling actual human behavior—I told her I'm not going to run away. I was going to stay and fight. We enjoyed romantic bliss, again. Cue the nausea. Vomit from the Jameson.

Mistake #5

We made a new plan.

This plan called for complete sacrifice—from her. She would bide her time in Chicago as a lame-duck resident. I would go back to Los Angeles and pick up my life as if nothing had changed, save for the fact I would be talking on the phone more late at night. As late as it was for me, it was two hours later for her—and she had the job that started at nine. I made my own hours and frequently didn't put on pants until one p.m.

Three months later, I flew back to Chicago to pick her up and drive cross-country together. We stopped in Sedona, Arizona, and got so high we slept through New Year's. That was fun. And not technically a mistake, though I believe we did have dinner reservations and that is a very uncool thing to do on New Year's Eve.

We arrived in L.A., but not to live together. (This is a mistake within the larger mistake, but not necessarily one that warrants its own number.) I helped her find an apartment a few blocks away with a friend of mine, convincing her this gave us something to look forward to—a step to take together. I will admit, at this point I was starting to believe my own bullshit and, worse still, had lost the ability to determine what was bullshit and what was truth. Now, this is an easy call. Bullshit. The truth: I was afraid to live with her for fear of it not working out and feeling guilty that I dragged her all the way to L.A., only to have it end badly and now we live together and it sucks for everyone. In poker and the stock market this is called hedging your bets. In relationships it's called being a pussy.

Mistake #6

This really is the killer and I will say all the others can be dismissed as mistakes only in retrospect. They are situation specific, original, and unprecedented. This, however, is a really stupid thing I did and something I *should* have known not to do. I introduced her to all my friends and encouraged her to hang out with them on her own. Now, the operative word here is *all*. *Some* is fine. *Many* is all right. *Just about every one* would be okay, too. But not *all*. Not the ones you *know* are dodgy. Not the ones whose dodginess you have personally witnessed for years. A dodginess legendary amongst his contemporaries. That's just buying a ticket for an express train to Crushtown.

The Dumping and the Damage Done

We drift. We don't break up, but we don't try too hard to address issues either. She tried. I know I tried to try. One time we were in a car with my dad and he mentioned casually how his mother died. Turns out I never knew. I was embarrassed because

I was twenty-six and you should probably know this kind of stuff at that age. Especially since by my standards my dad and I had a "good" relationship. According to Jill, that was "telling." I thought about trying to turn my emotional retardation into a plus. "Won't it be exciting to watch me grow up before your very eyes? And there's nothing illegal about sleeping with an emotional pre-teen!" Alas, I didn't know how to talk to her. Or at this point, if I even wanted to.

Time to take stock of the relationship. Not together. That would have been foolish. I decided to go someplace exotic, but not too exotic so as to undercut the weight of all the stock-taking. I chose Scotland. I had some friends in Edinburgh and I could go and wander around soft mossy hills, awash in sheep dung and low clouds. I went in the dead of winter, so there were only five or six hours of light per day. Then I went to the northernmost part of the country, as if I was trying to escape the revealing light of the sun itself. This added gravity—especially since I was the only person in all the hotels I stayed at. Do you get it? I was alone. Isolated. A four-year-old could psychoanalyze what I was doing! I thought long and hard about where we were at. What I wanted. What was fair. What was right. I also spent a good deal of time wondering why they call eggplant *aubergine*. That's just way too fancy a word for, let's be honest, a pretty shitty vegetable.

Soon after I returned to the States, a letter arrived. It was from one of my best friends—the dodgy one—telling me he had developed strong feelings for and was now in love with my . . . I guess *ex*-girlfriend. The letter made no explicit mention of "bath" time, but it wasn't difficult to imagine.

What followed wasn't pretty. Letters and accusations flew. On more than one occasion I uttered the words "I would rather starve than eat your bread." (Thanks for the assist, Pearl Jam!) Gifts and baubles were repackaged and left on doorsteps. Not a small thing, considering one such gift was a decoupaged coffee table. That bitch was heavy.

Then the sadness. Prolonged, boring, mopey. Plotted countless acts of revenge. Odd how there's no plural for the word
revenge itself. I wanted *revenges*. And not of the "living well"
variety, either. I longed for calamity. Locusts. Fire and brimstone.
A pox on their house and cars that gave them endless mechanical
problems. But mostly I felt bad for myself. Overly bad, like "I've
been martyred on a cross of two people I had dared to trust"
bad. I admit here and now, I started writing poetry as an outlet.
Buried somewhere in a storage facility or a basement thick with
spiderwebs and creaky ski boots is a yellowed legal pad with the
words "The Night Table Years" scribbled on the first page. When
I die, someone will find it, be momentarily excited, then read it,
and then, I hope, burn it.

Years passed before I found myself in something even
remotely resembling a serious relationship. Self-mythologically
speaking, I'd say it was because it just took me that long to find
someone I actually cared about. In reality, I was broken and dis-
interested. Also, that whole thing about L.A.'s hyper-Darwinian
mating scene. Tough nut to crack.

Jill and I didn't meet cute and we certainly didn't break up
neat. In fact, we never saw or spoke to each other again. But in
the years that followed, I came to realize it most certainly wasn't
all her fault. In fact, it may be no more appropriate for her to ask
for my forgiveness than it is for me to ask for hers. But I'm the
one writing, so I get to do both. And, in the same way military
cadets eventually thank their drillmasters for their cruel tute-
lage, I offer my gratitude. Everybody gets crushed. For the lucky
ones it only happens once.

Lesson #19   You Can Encapsulate Feelings of Regret, Panic, and Desperation in a Two-and-a-Half-Minute Pop Song

by Adam Schlesinger,
Professional Songwriter

As a professional songwriter, it is my job to vividly portray the minutest details of human relationships quickly and accurately. Complex emotions must be captured in a few simple couplets. How, you ask, can this be done? Well, first one must have something meaningful to write about. And then one must learn The Craft.

Of course, I would NEVER use my own life experiences as the basis for my own songs. My songs are 100 percent fiction. But by carefully observing others, I have developed a keen sense of human psychology. Also, I have mastered the use of rhyme, various poetic devices, and even "slang," which I employ occasionally to give a lyric a "tossed-off" quality. The end result is that I am able to create strikingly realistic character voices in song; so realistic, in fact, they are often mistaken for me.

Annotated below are the lyrics to the song "Baby I've Changed" (once called "one of the greatest B-sides of the last four weeks" by the University of Cincinnati *News-Record*). And, though the voice of "me" in the song may often seem to actually be ME, remember that it is only a character . . . a carefully constructed illusion.

BABY[1] I'VE CHANGED[2]

She used to love me
But she don't love me no more[3]
I stepped over the line too many times
And she stepped out the door[4]

But baby I've changed
Won't you come back home[5]
'Cause I've changed my wicked ways[6]

And I'll never throw your mail away[7]
And I won't tell you that your hair looks gray[8]
And I'll let you listen to Sugar Ray[9]
And I'll say I love you every day[10]

'Cause it's true
Baby I do

Now I hope and I pray[11]
I can turn this mess around[12]
And I search for a way to convince you to stay
And not just skip town[13]

'Cause baby I've changed
Won't you come back home
'Cause I've changed my wicked ways

And I'll put away my socks and shoes[14]
If the lights go out I'll change the fuse[15]
And I'll let you listen to the blues[16]
And I'll say I love you just because it's true

Baby I do
Baby I do[17]

1. "Baby" is a term of endearment often used in popular song. See also: Bread, "Baby I'm-a Want You"; The Miracles, "Ooh Baby Baby."
2. For the careful reader, the title reveals this song is clearly a work of fiction. Because people don't change.
3. When expressing heartfelt sentiments in lyric form, it is permissible to use incorrect grammar, according to the Recording Industry Association of America. The slangy nature of the phrase "she don't love me no more" implies that the narrator is too overcome by heartbreak to remember how to speak proper English.
4. Note the clever contrast of the metaphorical "step[ping] over the line" with the literal "step[ping] out the door." Any song examining the end of a relationship should include a vivid description of the physical act of leaving. See also: Simon, Paul, "50 Ways to Leave Your Lover," in which the character Jack is advised to "slip out the back," while a certain Gus is counseled to "hop on the bus." (The exact nature of the relationship between Jack and Gus is left undefined.)
5. The song's crafty protagonist hints that "home" for his departed lover is the place they shared, and not, in fact, her sister's couch in Westfield, N.J.
6. Alliteration is, according to *Wikipedia*, a poetic device which "contributes to the euphony of the passage, lending it a musical air" and may also "add a humorous effect."
7. This does not imply that he had ever previously thrown her mail away. Tampering with or discarding someone else's mail is a federal crime and is in no way endorsed by the songwriter or this book's publisher.
8. When in a relationship, it is important to phrase physical observations about your partner in a positive manner. Instead of pointing out that some of her hair is gray, for example, our protagonist could have complimented her on the fact that most of her hair is not gray.
9. With this major concession, our narrator reveals the true depths of his commitment and the level of sacrifice he is willing to make in order to salvage the flagging relationship.
10. Mumbling "love you too" occasionally, as when ending a phone call, is here acknowledged to be insufficient as a verbal expression of true passion.
11. The subject of faith is often addressed indirectly in popular music, in order to appeal to religious audiences without alienating the more mainstream "hedonist sinner" market.
12. "Mess" here refers to the situation at hand, and not to the former lover herself.
13. "Skip town" is another slang term, defined by the *Urban Dictionary* as "to move to another city/neighborhood when your house/crib gets shot up by a rival gang."
14. Although it is unlikely that the main reason she left was the sight of his shoes, he is presumably just trying to cover all his bases at this point.
15. In fact, they had circuit breakers, not fuses, but this did not rhyme.
16. "The blues" is a genre of music created by actors Dan Aykroyd and John Belushi and heard primarily in sports bars and at corporate events.
17. By repeating the phrase "I do" loudly as his final plea, the song's narrator perhaps hopes to be overheard by a passing justice of the peace, who will then marry him to his ex on the spot before she has time to realize what's happening.

Lesson # 20   I'm Easy

by Paul Simms

Well, well, well. Just look at you, walking into this dreary bar and lighting the place up like the noonday sun at midnight, twirling a lock of your long auburn hair pensively as you search the room—for what? For a soul mate, perhaps?

(I know, I know—I hate that phrase, too. Maybe that will end up being one of those things we both hate.) Maybe a few weeks from now, lying in your bed on a Sunday morning, I'll ask you, "What's your least favorite word or phrase?," and you'll say, "'Soul mate,'" and I'll laugh till you say, "What? Tell me!," and I'll tell you how I knew that from the moment I first laid eyes on you, and then we'll have sex again.

But I'm getting ahead of myself. You haven't even noticed me yet. That's okay, I can wait.

Maybe when your gaze settles on me, and we lock eyes in that mutual Hitchcockian tunnel-vision effect where the camera is, like, pushing in at the same time it zooms out, or however they do that, you'll come sit down next to me and we'll—

Now you've spotted the friends you came to meet. They look like good friends.

Maybe they'll be my friends, too.

Our friends.

Your eyes just came to life like emeralds lit by subterranean torches, and as you move across the room toward your friends you shriek at them, "What the fuck is up, yo?," in a voice so piercing that the entire bar goes silent for a moment, and I have to check my glasses to make sure the lenses didn't crack. You continue to bellow your every utterance (including the lines "Jägermeister is the bomb, dawg!" and "Just 'cause I'm a white girl don't mean I don't got some serious junk in the trunk!" and "Random! Random! Random!"), and the bartender leans in and whispers something to his bar back, and they look at you and laugh.

You must be a regular here.

(*Duration of crush: seventeen seconds.*)

❀   ❀   ❀

Oh my. What have we here? A rainy night in the city has cleared the sidewalks of all but the most intrepid pedestrians, and those who didn't brave the elements have no idea what they're missing.

Because there you are, gliding along on your bicycle, just a few feet ahead of me.

You're obviously not one of those tedious hard-core cycling enthusiasts—no skintight black spandex for you. No, just a simple white T-shirt (soaked through to the skin, clinging to the small of your back) and a long blond ponytail, whipping back and forth like the tail of a cartoon pony, as those long legs of yours pump the pedals and you raise your face to the sky, letting the raindrops freckle your cheeks with sweet diamonds of moisture.

Dare I try to catch up to you? I'm on foot, carrying a bunch of shopping bags, but you've paused at a red light, and—what the heck? I don't know what I'll say to you, but even the clumsiest of introductions on these glistening nighttime streets will give us a romantic how-we-met anecdote that we'll love telling for years to come.

Caught you! Here I am!

And there you are. I see now that you're a dude. My mistake. It was the ponytail that threw me off.

(*Duration of crush: thirty-three seconds.*)

        ✿   ✿   ✿

Another restaurant dinner with my boring girlfriend, another lecture about how I never really listen to whatever she's yammering on about.

But how can I listen—how could anyone?—when across the room, alone at a table, reading the newspaper and nursing a glass of white wine, is a silent confection like you?

You, with your jet-black hair (like a latter-day Veronica from *Archie*) and your skin so pale that the bubble-gummy pinkness of your pouty lips seems almost obscene, especially when you scrunch them up the way you do every time you lick your forefinger and turn the page.

And I know you see me, too. Your first glance betrayed a glimmer of recognition—as if you knew me but couldn't remember from where—followed by puzzlement, your eyes entreating me to silently remind you, which I couldn't do at the time because my current girlfriend was staring across the table at me, apparently waiting for my answer to some kind of relationship question that I thought was rhetorical.

And so it goes. For an eternity, it seems—through the entire meal, until I watch you ask for the check, and pay it, and get up to walk out of the restaurant, and my life, forever.

But what's this? You're crossing the room toward me? So brazen—just as I knew you'd be. Are you going to surreptitiously slip me your number, written on a sugar packet, perhaps dropping it in my pocket as you fake-jostle me, like a spy handing off microfilm?

My heart beats like underwater thunder in my ears, until you tap my girlfriend on the shoulder, and she sees you and says,

"Hey!," and you say, "I thought that was you!," and I realize that you are one of my girlfriend's college roommates.

After you leave, my girlfriend tells me a hilarious story about how one time in college some guy broke up with you, so you found some photos of him nude with the word *Patriarchy* written on his chest in Magic Marker which you took for an art class, and you sent them to his parents and then posted them on your blog, where you apparently like to write incredibly detailed confessionals about the asshole guys you always end up dating, and also, while you don't use the guys' real names, everyone knows that the guy you immortalized as Pencil Dick is actually a guy I used to work with.

(*Duration of crush: forty-five minutes.*)

❋ ❋ ❋

So silly does my impatience now seem, stuck as I am in the Starbucks line during the morning rush. But that was before I noticed you in line ahead of me.

And now that I've seen you—with your gossamer hair still damp from the shower, with your well-moisturized ankles strapped and buckled into high heels that make you wobble and sway like a young colt just finding her stride, with your scent of lilacs and Dial, and, most of all, with your infectious sense of calmness and serenity, which makes me wish that the world itself would stop spinning, so that gravity would cease and we two could float into the sky and kiss in the clouds, giddy with love and vertigo—

Now you're at the register, and the dreaded moment when we part without meeting rushes toward me like a slow-motion car crash in a dream.

You've been at the register without saying anything for, like, fifteen seconds now, still scanning the menu board with those almond-shaped eyes that would make Nefertiti herself weep with envy.

Seriously, you've been to a Starbucks before, right? I mean, it seems like there are a lot of choices, but most people find a drink they like and stick with it. And order it quickly.

But maybe I've caught you on a day when you've decided to make a fresh start. To make a fresh start, to try a new drink, to walk a different way to work, to finally dump that boyfriend who doesn't appreciate you.

Okay, even if that were the case you could have picked out your new drink while you were waiting in line, right? I mean, come on.

Well, you've won me back, my future Mrs. Me—by turning to me and mouthing, "Sorry," after you finally noticed me tapping my foot, looking at my watch, and exhaling loudly. Sensitivity like that can be neither learned nor taught, and it's a rare thing indeed. The rarest of all possible—

Jesus Christ, you've ordered your drink and paid; do I really have to stand here for another forty-five seconds while you repack your purse, the contents of which you've spilled out on the counter like you're setting up a fucking yard sale or something?

That's right, the bills go in the billfold, the coins go in the little coin purse, the billfold and the coin purse go back in the pocketbook—no, in a side pocket of the pocketbook, which seems to have a clasp whose design incorporates some proprietary technology that you haven't yet mastered.

I think I hate you now.

(*Duration of crush: five minutes.*)

Things More Majestic and Terrible Than You Could Ever Imagine

by Todd Hanson

We are told the healthiest way to think about life's seemingly near-continual parade of tragedy, pain, and humiliation is to view each of these defeats as a learning experience—"Whatever doesn't kill me makes me stronger," as the saying goes. Technically, that's not true—multiple sclerosis, an inoperable disability, or a nonfatal debilitating injury that results in permanent brain damage are just a few of the examples I could name—but let's just pretend it's true for the sake of argument.

IF getting dumped is a learning experience, it is fair to say I've not only earned several PhDs, but also put in an impressive amount of postdoctoral work as well. So, alas, there is no way I could explain everything I've learned, not in the space provided here nor even in the remaining years I have on this planet.

Of these truths I have learned, some were so fantastic I never would have thought them possible if I hadn't experienced them myself. Others, so soul-searingly awful they beggar description. Still more fall into a Nietzsche-esque "Beyond Good and Evil" category that defies classification altogether.

What follows, therefore, are three unbelievably abbreviated lists—a highlight reel; a mere overview, if you will, of a vast, unwanted body of knowledge.

Things Positive

1. That high school girlfriend you dated so long your young, naïve self is desperate to break up with her, but has such a hold on you you can't seem to get away no matter what you do? Don't worry—you won't be stuck with her forever after all.

2. The average Midwestern liberal-arts campus has, it so happens, at least one budding young radical feminist who, despite her vocal opposition to patriarchal hegemony, diatribes against "the male gaze," and propensity for declaring herself a lesbian every couple of months, is nonetheless so mind-blowingly sexy that every single guy on campus wants desperately to get into her pants. When you meet this girl, you will assume you have absolutely no chance of ever doing so. Good news: you're wrong!

3. Sex with heavily tattooed punk-rock drummer chicks whose breasts bounce hypnotically as they hammer away onstage is pretty much as amazing as you'd imagined. I cannot emphasize this point enough.

4. Fantasy celebrity women you've seen on TV—the kind who are in relationships with major movie stars and live in mansions in the Hollywood Hills—are, it's fair to assume, permanently relegated in your brain to the "That'll Never Happen" category. In fact, going out with one is so outside your range of expectations, you probably wouldn't believe it was happening *even if you were in the middle of actually doing so.* But guess what? Wrong again!

5. There exists a certain type of busty Manhattan redhead that makes the girl from those classic Tex Avery cartoons—you know the one, the showgirl that causes the cartoon wolf to spin cartwheels, shoot steam out his ears, and flail helplessly as his animated eyeballs pop out and go rolling across the floor?—look less like a comical cartoon

exaggeration than an example of the Italian cinematic school known as *Neorealismo*. No, I'm not making this up.

Things Negative

1. That intense desire you felt to be free of your long-term high school girlfriend can turn, overnight, into an unbearable eight-month fit of jealousy, rage, sobbing, and self-pity, just by finding out, post–high school, that she has been sleeping with the pot dealer from her dorm. Who knew?

2. Falling in love with someone every other guy on campus is *also* in love with can make you feel better about yourself than any antidepressant ever concocted by modern science. But, you'll discover, it also has its *disadvantages*—like the fact that at any given moment there are twenty-thousand-odd guys waiting to go out with her the instant she dumps you. This is a situation she will feel no compunction about taking full advantage of with no warning, whenever the whim strikes her.

3. Punk-rock drummer chicks are considered wild and unpredictable for a reason. They can fall head over heels for you, but if you aren't up to speed, they can just as easily— mere days after declaring they can't stand to be without you—pull a complete 180 and get back together with their ex, even if said ex happens to be on really dangerous street drugs at the time.

4. Spending the night with a fantasy celebrity woman you've seen on TV and looking over and realizing the decidedly male items littering the nightstand on your side of the bed belong to the major movie star she is "still in the process of breaking up with" is far less glamorous, and much more stressful, than you'd think. And being told the following morning over breakfast, repeatedly, that she "can't wait to see you next" doesn't mean you'll actually

ever hear from her again—even if she continues to flirt with you every time you run into each other over the next several months. Far from being an ego boost, the experience can leave you as confused about the very fabric of reality as Philip K. Dick writing his fabled *Exegesis*— and like him, you will never be able to convince yourself you'd didn't just hallucinate the whole thing.

5. As talented, funny, and fabulous as they may be, sometimes flabbergasting Manhattan redheads call you up at midnight and demand you take a cab from Brooklyn to Manhattan, so they can yell at you until four a.m. about how they need to break up with you because you're too emotionally inaccessible to make a commitment. Even if you've only seen each other, like, *twice*. What's more, though they've decided they despise you with every fiber of their being, this is somehow no guarantee the relationship will actually end there.

6. There is a saying in the entertainment industry: "Faster, better, cheaper—you can only have two." Unfortunately, this same principle applies to romantic partners, with the corresponding categories of sexy, smart, and sane. The tendency of some (me) is to go for the first two and damn the torpedoes. The consequences of doing so, however, can be more emotionally nightmarish than an H.P. Lovecraft story, crossed with a Manson Family acid trip, and directed by David Lynch.

7. That last sentence may have come across as hyperbole. Actually, it was a drastic understatement.

Things Indeterminate

1. Strangely enough, after a surprisingly brief elapse of time, you will no longer give two shits about the high school girlfriend you were once so devastated about you

dropped out of college. It may seem like a happy ending that it was no big deal after all—until you realize this means you dropped out of college *for absolutely no reason*, which is an even more depressing conclusion to live with for the rest of your life.

2. Just because hot college chicks are capable of dumping you on a whim doesn't mean they aren't capable of *reuniting* on a whim too. This feels great—until they dump you on a whim *again.* But hey—then they can take you back on yet another whim! This cycle can continue for not one, not two, but *five years* . . . until you have firmly established a love/hate codependency not dissimilar from the Miami economy's relationship with cocaine.

3. There are, always, *other* punk-rock chicks, fantasy women, and brassy redheads (to say nothing of the actresses, lawyers, writers, and vegan PETA activists) out there that you *haven't even met yet.* Waiting, somewhere in the darkness, for you to fall in love with one day. On the one hand, this is as good a reason as you'll ever have to get down on your knees and thank God for His eternal benevolence. On the other, it is valid cause to rend your garments and curse His holy name. This is neither good nor bad; like most aspects of the human condition, it is both.

4. That whole Icarus-flying-too-near-the-sun-and-plummeting-out-of-the-sky thing? That's real. Same with the Sirens who lure you to death with their irresistible song, and the odalisque so beautiful anyone who looks at her dies. And remember: as badass as Grendel was, Beowulf hadn't seen anything until he went up against Grendel's *mother.* I know, I know—I thought they were just myths too. But the fact is, sometimes, if you don't want to meet with a tragic end, your only option is to avert your gaze, tie yourself to the mast with cotton in your ears, or ascend a little less close to the Vault of Heaven.

❖   ❖   ❖

The sad fact is, there are more ways to get rejected than you ever dreamed. You can get rejected by women who don't like you enough and by women who like you too much. You can get rejected by women you didn't even know you were going out with in the first place. And you can even get rejected by women for not rejecting them. But remember, though it's counterintuitive, basic logic dictates that any time a relationship that *should* and *does* end, it is always, by definition, a good thing . . . even if it make you feel like tearing off your own head and angrily hurling it into oncoming traffic.

It is also crucial to bear in mind that even after a lifetime of such learning experiences, *you will never understand the first thing about women.* Do not delude yourself about this. Guys who claim to understand everything about women are like Kansas school boards that claim to understand everything about the creation of the world—interesting from a sociological perspective maybe, but still, totally full of shit.

And of course, none of the above changes in any way the larger, overriding fact that women have always been, are, and will eternally remain the Official Most Awesome Entities Ever Bestowed Upon Undeserving Mankind. Thus, despite my vast experience *getting* dumped, the number of times *I* have dumped someone else is, as of this writing, holding steady at exactly zero. Being what is sometimes euphemistically referred to as "the sensitive type," I guess I know how it feels too well to bring myself to do that to somebody else— even in cases where it clearly would have been not only the smartest course of action, but also the most humane.

I am showing improvement, however: my last two relationships ended *mutually.* It is truly wonderful to be me!

Lesson #37 Always Make Her Feel Like She's #1

"Distracted? Oh, Come on—I was using the hands-free headset!"

Lesson # 38   Dirty Girls Make Bad Friends

by A. J. Jacobs

As with every man in America—even Jake Gyllenhaal—I've had many unrequited crushes over the years. They're painful. Horrible. But, worse still, I've also suffered repeated exposure to a special subset of unrequited crush. And it is, I believe, the cruelest variety. Namely, unrequited crushes on women who talk dirty. As in, women who are dreaded "just friends," but who discuss with you in vivid detail their exploits with other men who are not "just friends." Avoid this situation. It is hell in its purest form—a constant and excruciating reminder of that which you will never experience.

In college, there was Anya—a striking Sandra Bullock look-alike from Portland. Anya took a lot of classes on human sexuality and enjoyed telling me the content of those classes, including how they related to her life. I'd listen intently, nod my head, then spend the next half hour digging my fingernails out of my leg. Anya eventually became a noted sex researcher and wrote a book on her year of living with the girls at the Mustang Ranch brothel in Nevada. (Fun Fact: If you want a threesome with a black and a white woman, just ask for the "Salt and Pepper Special.")

Years later, as part of my job as an editor at *Esquire* magazine, I oversaw the sex column, which was written by another impossibly attractive woman. Every week or so, we'd have long, intense phone discussions about, for instance, why lesbians in porn movies seem to enjoy fellating dildos. Then I'd hang up and furiously edit an article on how to write a thank-you note or the world's best golf umbrella—anything to calm down.

Those were tough, for sure. But my most agonizing experience with a bawdy girl was with my friend Chloe. We met in college, but started hanging out in earnest after graduation, when we were both living in New York and severely underemployed. She was hard to miss: Blond hair that was seriously blond, like the color of a smiley face sticker. She wore a massive silver *Playboy* pendant, cowboy hats, tiger-skin pants, enormous pink sunglasses—shirts and dresses all with plunging necklines. Her theory being if you look and act like a celebrity, you will eventually become one. She was basically an early version of Nicole Richie, but with a high IQ and no trust fund. And it worked—a little. She did start to hang out with the famous, or at least to inhabit the fringes of celebrity culture. You can spot her as one of the official "hot girls in the background" of the opening credits of early-nineties *Saturday Night Live*.

She was funny and smart and outrageous and let me tag along with her everywhere—to bars that were too hip for me, parties that were too hip for me, concerts that were too hip for me. We once went to the Catskills together, and when I was with her, it seemed the Catskills were too hip for me too.

I was smitten. She was not. But she was no prude. She was quite romantically adventurous with other men. And she liked to tell me about those romantic adventures.

She told me about how this indie film director was performing oral sex on her the night before and, while he was doing it, he made her call her mom and discuss Thanksgiving plans. It gave him some sort of perverse Freudian thrill. The sick bastard. The sick, lucky bastard.

She told me about how, when she was in Florence, Italy, she got drunk at a café, and at the next table was a famous network sports anchor who was even more hammered. They, of course, ended up messing around in the restaurant bathroom.

She also had a weakness for musicians. It killed me. How could she fall for that cliché? Why not a weakness for something more original . . . say, Boggle players? Or guys who've read every Hercule Poirot mystery? Or men with moles on their face? That'd give me a fighting chance. (And not just because I have a giant mole on my face and can quote Poirot chapter and verse.)

But no, she went ahead and had flings with guitarists and lead singers, probably a drummer or two. I'd never heard of any of the bands these guys were in, but apparently they were well known to people who read *Paper* magazine and rented walk-ups in Alphabet City.

So I'd listen to the stories of her escapades. And I'd pine. For those who've never endured this particular torture, how can I describe it? It's like sitting at a restaurant while the waiter describes the mouthwatering specials—then returns to say they're all no longer available. (Oh, and by the way, the restaurant is out of food altogether. And you have to go in the back and help with dishes. And you won't get paid.) Or maybe it's like the dot-com boom. This was the midnineties, after all. Every day I'd read about another twenty-two-year-old who sold his online turtle aquarium company for a quarter billion, while I scraped by on a journalist's salary, sucking down the bitter cocktail of jealousy, longing, and regret.

I can't say for sure why I kept coming back to the dirty gals. Partly, I think, bad luck. But partly, the maddening fact that these women all tended to be interesting and funny.

With Chloe, I tried this tactic: Whenever she'd talk about her boyfriend du jour, I'd try to come up with all the reasons she and I would make a terrible couple. She was a commitment-phobe. I could have been happily married at twenty-two. She'd stay out till four every night. I don't like going outside, unless it is to evacuate a burning building. She loved going to earsplitting concerts. I got cranky when NPR was on too loud. A valiant attempt, but it didn't work.

What made it worse was that everyone assumed we were a couple. Even my family. When I wasn't dating anyone—which was not uncommon—I would take Chloe to family functions, which always resulted in a similar scene. We'd walk in—Chloe would be wearing, say, a cleavage-bearing baby T, a micro-mini-skirt, and knee-high black leather boots—and she'd whisper to me, "Everyone's staring at me."

"Naaah," I'd say.

Then I'd look around and, well, yes they were. In fact, they all would have their eyebrows raised like Spencer Tracy when Sidney Poitier entered the dining room. One time, my aunt gathered up enough courage to ask Chloe about her wardrobe. Chloe explained that she sees getting dressed every morning as a chance to put on a costume.

"Ohhhh, I understand," said my aunt. It finally made sense to her: She is not an *actual* prostitute. She just puts on a costume that makes her look like one.

Chloe encouraged me to date other women, which was hard when she was around, since Chloe could be an intimidating, cleavage-bearing presence. One time, she prodded me into my first pickup attempt at a bar. Here's the quick version: We spotted an attractive brunette drinking Dos Equis with a couple of friends. "Come on," said Chloe. "Let's go." She would be my wingwoman.

We approached, and Chloe engaged the woman in a conversation. After a minute—and I can't remember how it came up—we learned that both the brunette and I were born in 1968. Now, 1968 happens to be pretty much the worst year in American history: the assassinations of Robert Kennedy and Martin Luther King, the Tet Offensive, and on and on. So whenever my birth year came up in conversation, I would comment, "Such a wonderful year, 1968. So proud I was born then." At which point I'd list all the horrible things that happened. It's not Noël Coward, but I'd usually get a mild chuckle. So I tried it out.

"Such a wonderful year, 1968. The assassination of Martin Luther King . . ."

And then I stopped. I lost steam. I'm not 100 percent sure why. I think I realized the joke was iffy, so I bailed. It didn't seem appropriate for the first couple of minutes of conversation. Unfortunately, it was much less appropriate to stop where I stopped. The brunette recoiled, repulsed and frightened. She shot me a look, "Please don't kill me. Just go back to your Aryan Nation meeting." She walked away without another word. (I think it goes without saying, I have since retired that joke . . . and have never again spoken to strange women in bars.)

Maybe I unconsciously torpedoed the pickup attempt because I was so infatuated with Chloe. Something had to give. So one summer night, I finally made a pass at Chloe. It was the worst-planned, poorest-executed pass of my life. She was sleeping over at my apartment, as she did whenever she didn't want to schlep home. That very night I had been dumped by a mutual friend of ours. I thought the woman dumped me for another guy. But Chloe gently informed me that the other guy was gay, and my ex was bisexual, and they were at a gay club together as we were speaking. This is what happens when you go to a liberal arts college with no core requirements.

At the end of the night, we were watching TV, and I looked at Chloe and said, "I want to kiss you.'

"No. I don't think that's a good idea."

"Why not?" Perhaps I could debate her into it.

"I don't want to get involved in your love triangle. Or love square. Or love pentagon, or whatever it is."

Then she paused. "Love pentagon. That's almost an oxymoron."

"What?"

"The Pentagon is all about war, not love."

I was finally confessing my long-term crush, and she was doing wordplay. And not even good wordplay. I think it was the third whiskey sour talking.

What was clear was that this was not an emotionally wrenching moment for her. Awkward, yes. But not wrenching. It was probably the only sexual encounter we never talked about again. On that night, I finally snapped out of denial. I realized she would never like me. Never see me the way I saw her. It was at once painful and so staggeringly obvious. I should have known. But the dirty girls keep you hanging on. Every dirty story. Every dirty detail. You think, "That could be me."

Eventually, as could be scripted by Captain Obvious, Chloe ended up with a guitarist from an alternative band, and I married a woman who worked in magazines. We lost touch, partly because my wife and Chloe didn't mesh. (See the preceding 1764 words for the reason why.) But I still think about Chloe often. I am reminded of her when I see a certain famous sportscaster or catch an old episode of *Saturday Night Live*, or even hear about the Pentagon. But not, thank God, when I call my mother to discuss our Thanksgiving plans.

Being Awkward Can Be a Prophylactic Against Dry Humping

by Matt Goodman

That middle school is rough is a truism, but consider the pressures of the environment in this particular experiment: being a non-Jew in a school in full bloom bar mitzvah season, gold-foil-encrusted invitations and candle lightings at the Waldorf, me with my L.L.Bean tie and a bowl haircut, wishing for my nascent Jewish faith to awaken inside me; reading through *Guitar World*, learning the vernacular of licks and pick scrapes ("sizzling leads," "shrieking wail," "Malmsteen"), and then picking up my three-quarter-size acoustic guitar with the plinky nylon strings I find so embarrassing, piddling out a bare approximation of the intro to that Sublime song where he goes and shoots that *esse*; joining the soccer team and being the slowest, panting-est one there with the least spring in his kick, the one who is told "I'm going to fucking breeze by you, fatty" by members of the opposing team and then is fucking breezed by, wishing I could head the ball in from my penalty box, sending the orb across the entire pitch.

The list of things so familiar to me but not actually tangible in my life stretches on, from that ball that should have been kicked in the net, to the solo I should have played, to the whopping check from Aunt Esther in Bayside that should have been deposited in my bank account on my thirteenth birthday. Topping the list, however, is love, or dry humping, or both; the magical friction of preadolescent groins grinding against each other through tighty-whiteys and dress pants and skirts hiked up awkwardly but erotically, an elated carpet burn feeling after. Not that I'd know, me with my pants so high up (the socks thickly bunched around my ankles) and my otherworldly knowledge of R. A. Salvadore dark elf fantasy and the sand wyrms of *Dune*.

But I *could* know, with the right sort of girl! The kind who wears her acne like a badge, who listens to Moxy Fruvous and wears Doors T-shirts with the logo in Hebrew, who naturally gives off a rank smell I'd recognize years later as patchouli. She is apeshit crazy. She demands to know if breasts would be as attractive to me if they were located on girls' stomachs instead of their chests. She watches *The Rocky Horror Picture Show* while talking about purchasing vibrators. She honks and snorts when she laughs, which she does at inopportune moments—moments of death or respect, though never moments of piety. She is deeply connected to her Jewish faith. She might just have a crush on me. I'm not entirely sure what it means when someone pins me to a couch and force-feeds me Twizzlers faster than I can chew them, red bits of licorice tumbling out of my furiously chomping jaws. She might like me, but that's not enough. I must win her love to make up for all the bar mitzvah after-party dry humping I've missed; for the goals, guitar leads, all of it. For vindication.

I, of course, can't do this by flowers or serenading, by movie tickets or even alcoholic social lubricant, because I know I'd fail at any of these endeavors. I'd go to a flower shop, spend ten minutes deliberating what to buy, and then give up and go home and cry into my pillow. I know the "opposites attract" adage, but being normal is impossible. So I pray that some wise man on a mountain plateau somewhere has another

aphorism, "identicals attract." This will yield a love, prefer-
ably carpet burn-y. I will win her not by following the well-
trod traditions of civil courtship. I can't quite do things
normally, but I certainly can be weird. Her crazy and my
derangement will spark and titrate and she'll be mine in all of
her oddball glory.

At least this is what I hope as I assemble by the buses at
the end of school. I'm half-invited to my crush's house and
accept wholeheartedly (half-inviting myself, completing the
invitation). To complicate things, two others are accompanying us to my crush's house. Or, truthfully, I am accompanying them, since they were invited wholly, no halves. One of
them asks me, "So why are you always looking down?" I
respond slowly, almost quizzically, "So I don't have to see
you?"

I get into her babysitter's car. The drive to Westchester is
all undulating hills and bushy trees. When I get there, I get
out of the car, but spend twenty minutes in her driveway on
scooters and skateboards. Eventually my crush gets bored,
and decides to head into the basement, full of colonoscopy
bags from her mother's practice. I sit on one of two brown
velvet love seats. One of the other two tries to sit down with
me. I shoo him away. They can sit on the other love seat.

My crush sits on me. She does not sit beside me in the
open seat, not even on the arm of the love seat, but on top of
me. She motions for Twizzlers, which I am then force-fed.
This is the woman for me, I think. This experiment will suc-
ceed. Love will precipitate. But we are interrupted by the
babysitter, who tells everyone to get into the car again. She
forgot to pick up my crush's little sister.

I am now idling in the SUV, across from the elementary
school. I watch children wait for their parents. My heart-
strings twang as my crush moves from the backseat, past the
middle row, and into the front seat, where she can operate

the stereo. Her breasts may have brushed my shoulder. This is love, I think. Maybe I should just take that elated tidbit and be content with it, but I am emboldened, ready to be apeshit crazy. Any moment now I'll jump into action, do something. Anything. Only problem is, I don't know what.

I fidget nervously as the other two, classic rock buffs, debate with my crush the merits of Ozzy Osbourne. I can feel every written word I've ever read about rock, about even just guitars, fade from my mind as I grasp for one liners about Led Zeppelin. As I haw about I watch one of the two make a move on my crush, putting an arm around her shoulder. I feel desperate. Ozzy Osbourne's "Crazy Train" rises from the speakers. Suddenly I'm stricken by the fear that my time to be apeshit crazy may be passing. I look around for opportunities and see a dog, what looks like a terrier-size German shepherd, squatting smack dab in the middle of the road—like, haunches at forty-five-degree angles to the yellow stripe, tail hovering parallel above it. The owner stands by, oblivious to whatever traffic might come along, fine with his dog brazenly defecating in the middle of the street. I fail to note a pooper-scooper in his hand. My crush and the flirtatious other are discussing whether Tony Iommi or Randy Rhoads was the better Ozzy sideman. I see vindication on the horizon. I think of one of my least favorite sayings, one goading me to action, any sort of action, before I lose my chance. Now or never.

I jump out of the SUV and begin running towards the dog. Everyone in the car watches, which encourages me. I will try and win over my crush by yelling at a dog in the middle of the street to stop defecating. I shriek "Stop crapping!" twice. I then bellow at the dog wordlessly, letting it know my sheer outrage that a dog would crap in the middle of the road. I am hoping this appeals to my crush's own inscrutable sensibilities. It was the best I could come up with.

My request succeeds as the dog, astonished, stops defecating and looks at me. Then the dog decides, as my crush is deciding, that I am a crazy kid, not in the fun way, but in the way that crosses the line, the awkward line that is painful to watch. The graceful avert their eyes and sigh. The chill of humiliation causes me to turn around, away from the dog and the man who is now demanding to know what I am up to. I heave a flimsy curse in his general direction and then walk briskly back to the SUV. I want to run, but need to walk in an attempt to salvage some, any, dignity.

It didn't work.

Before I despair, though, now that it's over, how bad was it really? How deep in my skin did it embed? It shouldn't have burrowed much, being a relatively minor event in that (a) while my love may have been spurned, she was perhaps too crazy to begin with or not crazy at all, and (b) it was embarrassing, but in front of a relative few. Three people aren't a big deal. Of course, my mind is infested with fears of "what if they tell someone," but for once I relish my anonymity within my school, my neighborhood. This invisibility gives me a grace period, to metamorph or incubate or simply jump from one point to another, to the socially viable person who can't remember how it happened and doesn't quite believe their own transformation. Besides, even if I insist that being horribly awkward and always rejected is my fate, I know that whole subcultures have sprouted for such people; depression is fetishized, commodified, gentrified even, and though being attached to a bunch of macabre-worshipers isn't a great idea, it might be nice to have some community. It might help.

We pick up the sister and drive back the house. Trying to redeem myself, I wait for someone to talk to me in the car, or in the driveway, or in the kitchen. No one does. I call my parents, who do, and on top of that will also come pick me up.

Thank God for parents. I leave the house without anyone noticing, departing their world leaving as little mark as I did coming in, besides, of course, for a slight depression on the love seat in the basement.

THE SORROWS OF YOUNG WALTER

OR THE LESSONS OF A CYCLICAL HEART

EVERY HEARTACHE WAS UNSOLICITED

BUT EVERY ONE BORE A RESEMBLANCE TO THE OTHERS

EVERY ONE RAN ITS COURSE...

A PERIOD OF CREATIVITY WOULD RESULT...

Dating a Stripper Is a Recipe for Perspective

by Patton Oswalt

Sometimes love goes wrong because your partner changes. Sometimes it fails because you change. But, more often than not, love fails because you stop appreciating what you've got. You grow complacent and bored. Quirks become annoyances. Thrills become chores. Novelty becomes drudgery. Who wants "safe" forever? Someone who will cherish you, understand you, grow with you, understand the areas where you don't mesh and react to that gulf with maturity and understanding—these are *exactly* the kind of people you become disenchanted with, and then leave, and *then* feel like a to-the-bedrock bastard for abandoning.

Sure, your journey of togetherness starts off all sprinkles and buttons. But even the sweetest apple plucked from the tree of love can become a rotted, flyblown failure full of disease, maggots, and yelling.

Yes, when love goes bad, it can fill an apple with yelling.

So how would you feel if I told you I can <u>guarantee</u> you a stable, healthy relationship? The kind of deep union wherein, upon waking each morning, you murmur a humble thanksgiving for the gift of eternal companionship, support, and love that's appeared in your life. And you never get bored. And you always appreciate it. Always. Always. Always.

The answer is quite simple, really. Date a stripper.

Strippers are our country's most precious resource for keeping people together, and humble, and happy. Forget about counseling. Forget about that weekend retreat to Sedona. And forget about self-help books featuring any of the following words: Secret, Code, Steps, Life, Love, Power, Triumph, or Borderline Personality Disorder.

Doubt me? Take these paired examples as all the proof you need:

Arguments

My wife at her worst:

Sometimes yells. Sometimes conflates one mistake I've made into a global condemnation of my character. When I point this out, she relents, laughs at herself, and apologizes.

My stripper ex-girlfriend at her best:

CHIVAS [*her stripper name, not her real name*]: You didn't introduce me to your friend.

ME: Whuh? [*It's 4:17 a.m., and she's woken me up.*]

CHIVAS: Two days ago. When we were on Larchmont and those people you knew came up. There were three of them and you only introduced me to two.

ME: Mike and Millie? Those were the only two I knew. I didn't know the third person, so I didn't know his name—it was a friend of theirs.

CHIVAS: WHAT THE FUCK WERE YOU THINKING WITH THAT MOTHERFUCKING MIX TAPE, YOU FAGGOT?

ME: What?!

CHIVAS: (*Louder, over the sound of her two pit bulls, both of which are now furiously barking*) I HATE ROXY MUSIC!

ME: What . . . what . . . wait . . .

CHIVAS: You think I like listening to that shit? Make a different fuck mix.

ME: Uh . . .

CHIVAS: Is that why you didn't introduce me to your gay friend on the street?

ME: What the fuck are you talking about? Why are you waking me up now?

CHIVAS: My dad molested me and my dogs hate you.

Finances

My wife at her worst:

Buys a lot of, in my opinion, overpriced skin care products.

My stripper ex-girlfriend at her best:

CHIVAS: So, you're going to start work in a movie next week?

ME: Yeah. It should be fun.

CHIVAS: I need to borrow some money.

ME: What for? You okay?

CHIVAS: My landlord is a Nazi Hitler.

ME: What's wrong?

CHIVAS: He's all like, "You haven't paid rent in five months, and if you don't cough up the money, I'm going to be a total Hitler and padlock your apartment."

ME: Why haven't you paid your rent?

CHIVAS: WHAT ARE YOU, MY DAD?

[*bark bark bark bark bark bark*]

Your Chance to be a Hero

My wife at her worst:

Sometimes sleeps until noon, depressed about a writing project that's stalled, and needs reassurance about her skills.

My stripper ex-girlfriend at her best:

CHIVAS: Where the *fuck* are you?

ME: I'm, uh, at work. It's Tuesday and I'm at work like I always am.

CHIVAS: The police in El Segundo are goddamn Nazi Hitlers.

ME: Oh.

CHIVAS: I need bail money.

ME: Holy shit, what happened?

CHIVAS: They let these old ladies with Alzheimer's disease drive school buses in El Segundo.

ME: Oh shit.

CHIVAS: And this bitch blocks the intersection suddenly, like out of nowhere, and now the front of my car is mulched and CAN YOU FUCKING GET DOWN HERE?!

SHERIFF IN BACKGROUND: Language.

CHIVAS: Oh, bite my clit you Naz–

Phone is hung up for her.

Extended Family

My wife's family, at their worst:

Typical kookiness and social awkwardness, alleviated by genuine charm, love, and understanding.

My stripper ex-girlfriend's family, at their best:

ME: You feeling okay?

CHIVAS: Yeah, sweetie.

ME: It's just that . . . I want you to know I'm here for you, and especially afterward, if things are uncomfortable. We can talk.

CHIVAS: What're you talking about?

ME: You know, what he did to you.

CHIVAS: And what *exactly* did he do to me?

ME: You said he molested you.

Chivas' father and his new girlfriend, who's younger than Chivas and looks almost exactly like Chivas, enter the Sizzler where we're meeting for dinner.

CHIVAS: WHAT THE FUCK ARE YOU TALKING ABOUT? WHEN THE FUCK DID I SAY THAT?

ME: Last n—

CHIVAS' DAD: What're you hollerin' about, doodlebug?

CHIVAS: He says I told him you fucked me!

CHIVAS' DAD: That was a nightmare you had! We agreed! [*To me*] Who the fuck are *you*?

CHIVAS: Who's *this* bitch?

CHIVAS' DAD'S GIRLFRIEND: Cowgirl with a bomb-ass pussy, that's who.

Chivas throws pepper mill at no one.

What it's All About, in the End

My wife at her worst:

Has taught me the past is dead, the future is uncertain, and all we can truly know, or come close to knowing, is the present.

My stripper ex-girlfriend at her best:

If you go down on a girl, or leave her a note saying you miss her, or don't pay her rent, you're a faggot.

❖   ❖   ❖

It only took two months of me dating a stripper to appreciate what a miracle my wife is. And I didn't meet my wife until three years after my stripper girlfriend's final, typo-heavy text message saying she was flying to "arJenteena" with a "music band." "Watch out for all the Nazi Hitlers!" I furiously texted back. Alas, she was gone.

I'd like to think she's still out there, perhaps not in arJen-teena, but somewhere else, Bolivia for example, giving some other poor fool a lesson he will never forget, and mentioning casually, in her own off-handed way, that her dad may or may not have molested her.

Lesson  42   # Sometimes You Find a Lost Love, Sometimes You Don't

by Bob Kerrey

In January 1961 at the beginning of my final semester of high school I put a photograph of a woman I loved in my wallet for the first and last time in my life. She had just won a skating competition. Head back, hair cut short, and smiling. She was beautiful but something about her captured me beyond her raw beauty. Nothing quite matched the spark, which arose between me and my girl, skating across the ice. The only problem was I had cut the photograph from *The Lincoln Journal* sports page. I had fallen in love with a total stranger. A very pretty one at that.

There wasn't much detail in the story accompanying the photo other than she was sixteen, a year younger than me. A month later she was featured on the front page of *Sports Illustrated* as the most promising U.S. female skater. Inside I learned that her older sister and both her parents were skaters and that her father had died when she was seven. I learned she was planning on attending college in the fall. Later, I learned—as I prepared to write about this lost love—that she and her mother had purchased several copies of *Sports Illustrated* right before boarding a plane bound for Brussels where she was to compete in the World Championships.

As it turns out, a wallet is the *least* safe place to put valuables. I didn't hold on to the photograph long. That summer my wallet fell into the warm water of a sandpit lake along the Platte River. The physical image was gone but the memory of her face has stayed with me to this day.

I thought of her when Darrel, one of my best friends, recently called to tell me about finding his lost love. Impressive, since Darrel is eighty-seven years old. His first wife died shortly after they celebrated their fifty-fifth wedding anniversary. His second divorced him after three years because he didn't act his age; he likes to swim in Puget Sound with the otters early every morning. (What is the proper age for early-morning swims with otters anway?)

The divorce depressed him and he began seeing a shrink "for the second time," he told me. Before long he was feeling better except that he was dating women who were in their thirties. I should say "because" he was dating women in their thirties. The shrink asked him about his past love life and Darrel told him about falling in love with his nurse when he was in the hospital for gallbladder surgery during the summer of 1963.

"That was when I went to a shrink for the first time. I asked him how much it would cost to talk me out of this [affair]. I did not want to destroy my family. I never saw her again."

For a man in love there are no more terrible words than those. I've uttered them too. In 1963 I called my girlfriend at the beginning of my third year in college. Her mother answered the phone and told me Sherry would not be coming back to school. "She's not Sherry Morse any longer; she's Sherry Poole. She got married this summer." I never saw her again. I would hope, if that were to happen now, I would at least get an e-mail.

Darrel's luck was better than mine, however. His second shrink suggested he try to get in touch with his long-lost nurse. He tracked down her address from a friend. She didn't answer him right away. Months later she told him her story. She had gone to college and had become president of a nursing college. She had been married but her husband had recently died. Their correspondence led to a meeting. Their meeting led to a decision to marry. (Have I mentioned Darrel was luckier than me?)

He was calling to tell me the good news. When I told him I had gone online to purchase a document certifying that I was a reverend so I could officiate the wedding of another friend, he asked if I would officiate his. So, this fall I will preside over the vows of the man who has, in turn, married me twice and baptized all three of my children. Technically, I still owe him a few.

Darrel and I became friends in 1973. The year we met was the year I started in business. It was the year I got engaged. It was the year a peace agreement was reached in Paris that allowed our prisoners of war to return home from Vietnam. We had a lot to talk about. We talked about the war and the poets who knew it best. I remember sharing Cummings' poem about "Olaf," a conscientious objector who while being destroyed kept repeating this perfection: "There is some shit I will not eat." It is a declaratory phrase I regret I learned too late.

We talked about love but did not trust ourselves to talk about our losses. These were too entwined with the dark and lonely places we shared with no one. Even the girl whose picture I removed from the newspaper remained a secret. My lost love and I never corresponded. We never met. The plane that took off from New York never landed in Brussels. It crashed killing all on board including my love, Laurence Owen, and the entire U.S. female skating team. I can still see her smiling face, sharp eyes, arched back, and confident spirit moving across the ice.

Don't Enter a Karaoke Contest Near Smith College; You Will Lose to Lesbians

by Jason Nash

When a man starts getting fine pussy, there's a boost to his ego unrivaled by anything else in life. Unlike getting a good job—which, when all is said and done, is still work—dating someone hot makes you feel intoxicated. Blessed. Like winning the lottery or even better, finding a massive discrepancy in your checking account. You don't know why you're getting all that money, but you keep your mouth shut and hope no one notices.

Karyn was the kind of beautiful I wasn't used to. Sort of alien looking, like a girl you'd see in a Prada ad, affecting a vacant stare while standing between two Wiemaraners. I always dreamed of dating a hot girl, but when I did, she didn't look anything like Karyn. Thanks to my mom's work in the cosmetics industry in the 1980s, my ideal woman has always been Samantha Fox, circa "Naughty Girls (Need Love Too)."

And Karyn was more than just unique looking. She was smart and said so very little, that when she did speak you would hang on her every word. She was impenetrable to trends, put absolutely no thought into her wardrobe, and was the first person I knew who admitted having horrible taste in music.

I saw her at the student union and I remember thinking, could I get this girl? Me? The guy who was a fat fuck in high school? The guy who was tormented for being the only Jewish kid and had the nickname "Wej"? (That's "Jew" spelled backwards.) The guy who ruined Thanksgiving dinner once when he put too much toilet paper in the bowl, leaving his aunt and uncle's shoes surfacing in an inch of shit water while they ate? That guy?

But things were going well for me in college. I had lost weight, had great friends, and scored an internship at *Saturday Night Live*. Most of all, I finally found my identity: the funny guy. The life of the party. And I loved it.

I approached Karyn at a bar. She was into me immediately, probably because I came highly recommended from a friend. I drove her home and we made out. It was goddamn heaven.

The final piece to my perfect college existence was there. A hot girlfriend. The only problem was, and I didn't realize it until years later, Karyn thought I was a fucking douche bag.

In fact, she may have *only* dated me because everybody else thought I was cool. To her I was a Britney Spears record, something of appeal but little substance that you look down at in line and go, "Why am I buying this?"

And the worst part was, I was a douche bag. I thought I was so cool back then. My jokes were terrible. I'd put a cigarette in my belly button and draw eyes and nose on my chest as a gag. Was I in fucking Mumenshantz? I tried so hard to get into the coolest bars on campus. I even dropped names about famous people I had met at *SNL*. Who could blame her for hating me?

That's not to say I didn't try to make her like me—even love me. Early on in our relationship I had an important realization: "Oh right, she hasn't seen me dance yet! Once Karyn sees what a good dancer I am, she'll give herself over to me completely."

I hatched a plan. I'd throw a party at my house, fully believing that once she saw my dancing ability things would turn around. Now, a word about my dancing. It is what I call "mock good." In that, no, it's not good, but I'm so serious about it I've convinced myself that it is good, and others seem to be charmed by that.

When the music came on I started moving and everyone began laughing and having fun. Everyone but Karyn, who just stood there, like a bored, unimpressed ice sculpture.

"Wait, no, you're not getting it," I wanted to say. "See, I'm being ironic. Notice me and appreciate the spectacle I'm making!"

I ran to her, trying to make it better but only doing more damage.

This, of course, is the curse of the insecure male. It's not our glasses or balding head. It's the fact that when the hot girl gets in our proximity, we simply can't just be. Our methods of survival are the very things that will drive her away.

It's like when you're at a fancy hotel pool and a bunch of girls take their tops off and it's no big deal. Well, I'm always the guy running to everyone else, pointing and yelling, "Did you see the topless girls? There are topless girls by the pool!" That's not what a guy with a hot girlfriend does.

The end came when I asked Karyn to come cheer me and a friend on in the finals of a regional karaoke contest. I would be singing "Say, Say, Say" and doing my best Michael Jackson impersonation.

"I don't think so," she sad. "That's your thing."

What the fuck did that mean? "That's your thing."

Karyn had this way of answering questions that would leave me unsure how she felt. "That's your thing." Like you're above my stupid college bar competition? Or like, you're jealous of my time in the spotlight? I mean, shit, girl, I wear a fucking sparkly glove during the song! Isn't that something you'd want to see?

Karyn never showed and we ended up losing to two lesbians who sang "Paradise by the Dashboard Light." The stage slid out underneath me during the best part of the song: where I come

come in with a lift of the leg and shake of the shin singing, "All alone I sit home by the phone! Waiting for you, baby!" It didn't matter really. The contest was a mile from Smith College. We never had a chance against those lesbians.

As we rode to the movies the next day, I was furious. I took a deep breath and finally said it.

"I don't get it. You don't think I'm funny. I mean, everyone thinks I'm funny but you."

"I know," she said, with no emotion in her voice.

We lasted a few months after that, mostly because I was living in New York. I drove back to college to see her, hoping she would be impressed by the fact that I had moved to the city. She wasn't.

Our sex started to go downhill, as she began not moving during the act. This made me unable to get hard, and then she blamed me for my lack of prowess. I was too much of a novice to tell her that half of this was her fault. I apologized repeatedly and convinced myself she had to have been molested at some point. Have I mentioned I was douche bag?

A few weeks later she dumped me. It annihilated me. I couldn't understand why she didn't like me. I had things going on. I mean, I cleaned David Spade's apartment! I thought about her every day for almost two years, and prayed she'd return. She did an amazing job of giving me nothing, never calling back and just letting me die, slow, cold, and painfully.

When I started writing this piece, I hired a private investigator in hopes of getting back in touch with her.

"Gonna be tough," said Detective Dave. "Single women in their late twenties, very transient group. Nothing holding them down."

I'm not chasing Sasquatch, asshole. Just put her name or social security number or something into the computer and tell me where she is. Three weeks later, Dave sent me an e-mail with a subject heading, "Well, We Did It!"

Dear Jason,

I made contact today with Karyn Gadd!

She called me to ask what this was about and I told her you wanted to talk to her for a short story. I told her that you had no ill feelings about the breakup and that you did not want to hurt her in anyway.

I DID give her your phone number, so CASE CLOSED.

Sincerely,

Dave Dineen, PI

Hey, Dave, maybe she would call me back if he didn't open with, "Hey, this guy's not going to rape and murder you, so why don't you give him a jangle."

And that was it. I was out $250 and she never called. Perfect really. The girl who never gave me anything, doesn't give it to me one final time. But what did I hope to hear? That I was obnoxious? That I was cheesy? That she started dating me because she thought I was cool, but quickly learned I wasn't?

Karyn made me realize my greatest fear: that someone would see through my tricks. My own personal David Copperfield bullshit I've honed to make other people think I'm special. And that's what she did, stripped me of anything valuable I had to offer.

More than her beauty, the thing I wanted most from Karyn was her calmness. Her ability to sit still, stare, and feel numb. I married someone equally as neurotic as I am and I love her and we make a very entertaining couple, but there is chaos everywhere we go. I slay dragons every day, or more to the point, I run from them, but I keep moving. Waiting, hoping one day I can rest and breathe easy. My wife is like Karyn in some ways. Smart, pretty, a tough audience. She hates when I need to be the center of attention. The difference is, I don't listen to her. I walk around every day positive I'm a good dancer.

Lesson 44 Get Dumped Before It Matters

by David Rees

Unlike most of the "winners" in this book, I've never been dumped.

Let that sink in for a moment: never been dumped. A perfect record. What's that thing in baseball, where batters are graded on some sort of numerical scale? Like, "Joe Smith is batting .300; he's hitting one out of every .300 balls." Well, when it comes to not being dumped, I'm batting 1,000.00. One thousand percent perfect. One thousand percent never-have-I-been-dumped.

You ask: "How did you get those awesome stats?" And, "Are your relationships available on baseball cards, so that I might learn from them?" And, "If so, what does the bubblegum taste like?"

The answers are, respectively, "Read on"; "Yes, from ToppsAdult"; and "Monogamy."

Although I am proud of my remarkable statistic, there's something you should know about it. Let's turn it over like a nursing sow and take note: How many relationships suckle at its teats? One and . . . two. Ah! You see, I'm not such an intimidating badass, I've only had two relationships: A girlfriend in high school and a wife, presently.

My high school girlfriend never dumped me. Or, whenever she did, I made sure to resuscitate our relationship and counterdump her down the line—effectively canceling out her dumps, which is how I maintained my perfect figure. (Like how -3 plus -3 winds up equaling +16, remember?)

That is to say, our relationship ended without the definitive, full-glottal stop of an asymmetrical dump. It was more like the slow, years-long decay of a mighty oak tree, where every few months a woodsman staggers by and makes out with the oak tree when he's tipsy, even though the better angels of his nature say, "Why complicate things in the forest, tipsy woodsman? Didn't you promise to stay away from that ol' oak tree?" And then the whole affair is immortalized in a mournful Appalachian fiddle tune.

Still . . . when all is said and done, I closed out my first "at bat" without getting dumped.

As for my second relationship, the one with my wife, things are starting to sound less like a mournful Appalachian fiddle tune and more like a Keith Moon drum solo being swallowed by a Cannibal Corpse song. Yes, sadly, my wife probably WILL dump me—and dump me hard, with extreme prejudice, like how Russell Crowe expresses his feelings in hotel lobbies.

The rub is, when you're a professional, grown-up man with a wedding band, a Roth IRA, and a funny feeling about that mole on your back; when you see all teenagers as irascible enemies of the state; when you start enjoying toast—when you get to that mature, married stage, it's not called "getting dumped." It's called "getting fucking divorced." And unlike getting dumped, getting fucking divorced ain't free. There's a whole legal element involved. Namely, you pay a lawyer to notarize your life as "Failure, Pending Lottery Win." He stamps your soul with his embossing machine so you can carry within you a legally binding bruise, for all time, to your grave, you colossal loser. Also, your tax return gets more complicated.

In short, divorce is an expensive, life-shattering, and inconvenient way to learn elementary lessons about life and love.

Lessons like these:

1. The fact that you mope around your "home office," sighing and scratching the five o'clock shadow spilling down your neck, while you "work on your screenplay in your mind," wearing sweatpants on a Wednesday afternoon, does not mean you are a tortured creative genius. It means you are a LOSER. If you're old enough to drive, you may no longer wear pants with drawstrings—even if they are your "dressy sweatpants." Look respectable for your woman, even while she's at work. It will comfort her to know you are wearing a belt. And by the way, if it's before noon, it's not called a "five o'clock shadow"—it's called a "shave, you loser."

2. The fact that you used to bake bread back in college, and now refuse to do so, even when your wife asks sweetly, longingly, does not mean you are a post-hippie citizen trying to carve out new paradigms of consumption in a post-9/11 world. It means you're lazy. Your depression has somehow turbo-charged your entropy. Congratulations! You are now the exact opposite of a Hadron Super Collider. If you don't act soon, and show some initiative in the kitchen, your molecules actually will leech out of your toes and stain your socks. Then you'll have to spend money on socks! Instead, bake a loaf of bread for your wife. In fact, shoot the moon and bake her a goddamn cake. She works much, much harder than you.

3. The fact that you spent approximately 40 hours last year watching *goddamn-can-you-believe-I-actually-did-this Miami Ink* does not mean you revel in the twenty-first-century agora as one node of the postmodern multitude. It means you have lost your mind and secretly want to die stupid. And alone. Turn off your television, unplug it from the wall, bury it under fifty pounds of sand in another country, and spend your evenings memorizing

seventeenth-century love poetry for your wife. Think about it—which will be more comforting in your twilight years: the collected verse of John Donne (WHICH YOU HAVE TOTALLY MEMORIZED) or vague memories of a bunch of tattoo-people talking about their feelings on TV?

Now that I appreciate the stakes, and understand how my shortcomings have flourished in the confines of my most important relationship, I have come to loathe my special statistic. I would happily trade my perfect dating record—that satiny, unblemished, unbedumpled sheet—for a mangy, flea-bitten patchwork quilt of "lessons learned," stitched together by women who dumped me.

I should have learned not to wear sweatpants from Siobhan, the vapid fashionista I should have met, and dated, and been dumped by, right out of college. Siobhan would have taken one look at my "awesome" collection of "exercise trousers" and had them secretly rendered to a base in Uzbekistan, where they would have been boiled alive. (My "special scarf" would have been water-boarded.) Then, when I met my wife for an anniversary cocktail I would have represented in a sleek pair of tailored slacks, not in paint-splattered Russell Athletics with the drawstrings hanging out over my crotch.

And Starshine, the free-spirited vegetarian carpenter I should have bumped into and dated in 1999 (and been spectacularly dumped by on the eve of the new millennium because of the Zodiac!), should have sat me down and reminded me that baking bread connects me to all humanity. For I am MAN, provider. Why deny this wretched world my gifts? If Starshine had done her job, my wife would be enjoying fresh-baked focaccia as I write this. Not frozen bagels made by robots.

Then, of course, there's Krystyn. Long-lost Krystyn. Lovely Krystyn. Sure, she had the world's worst name, and I sometimes called her "Kyrstyn" by mistake. (How we would have laughed about that!) But I still would have wept when she dumped me for watching too much television. I would still be haunted by her final words: "You watch too much television. I'm marrying Jaysyn, my X-treme athlete frynd. Because you watch too much television." I think that would have registered.

Alas, I have learned none of these things. Because none of those women existed.

You know those dummies with the black and yellow pie charts on their foreheads who are always smashing into windshields in slow motion? And in the slowed-down instant before impact, you can almost hear them say, in their mannequin drones, "Oh, I get it—I should have worn my seat belt?" I'm one of them, learning all these important lessons too late, in the melancholy split second before my head smashes through my marriage's windshield and bloodies any hope I had of eternal bliss.

I blame all the women who never dumped me.

It Wasn't Me, It Was Her

by Rick Marin

I got in touch with my college girlfriend recently when her husband left her for the daughter of a famous TV mogul. We exchanged e-pleasantries. Then she asked how come in my memoir, *Cad: Confessions of a Toxic Bachelor*, I didn't mention that she dumped me. Okay, Julia (as I called her in the book), I'll bite. I e-mailed back, "I thought I dumped you." Her response came fast and furious:

"Say you're joking or I'll lose what little faith in men I have left."

My fingers froze on the keys. I thought we were engaging in a few gentle jabs to the ribs, but she was serious. The woman was clearly in a vulnerable place, man-wise. A TV star in her own right in Canada, where we both grew up, she had now been reduced to tabloid fodder. I needed to be giving, sensitive, understanding . . . . Unfortunately, I possess none of these qualities. But I can be quite condescending.

"Well, if it was important for you to think that," I wrote, and changed the subject. Still, she'd planted the seed of doubt. Could my first love possibly have dumped *me*? For two decades, I'd firmly believed otherwise. You might even say I cherished the belief. Now I needed proof—a forensic analysis of the death of the relationship. Fingerprints, DNA, sunglasses like David

Caruso's on *CSI: Miami*. So I snapped on a pair of rubber gloves and went out to the garage to dig out a musty shoe box of Canadian-stamped letters with 1980s postmarks. Then I went into the musty shoe box of my mind (isn't that a Barbra Streisand song?) and dug out some memories of those years when I met the girl who almost became the first ex-Mrs. Marin.

It was my second year, Julia's first, at McGill University in Montreal. She had a wild mane of hair that a pretentious Art History 101 student (like me, then) might call "pre-Raphaelite." Her angular jaw-line was on a perfect parallel with her cheekbones. She had quick, appraising eyes and a slightly gummy smile with tiny perfect teeth. Big-boned, but toned, she was still coming into her looks and by no means thought of herself as the mediagenic beauty she would later become.

We met at a meet-and-greet in the quad of our dorm, Douglas Hall. I wasted no time in chatting up both her *and* her roommate. Julia would later profess amazement that this "short guy"—five feet nine, for the record—could be so cocky. Like most men, I went for the easier mark—the roommate. She was a blond innocent hot enough to have been wooed by Pierre Trudeau and chaste enough to have rebuffed his advances. I didn't get much further than Canada's playboy prime minister, but while I was trying, Julia and I became friends.

I was on the cocky side then, and she was the first woman I liked because she made fun of me. Her sense of humor was goofy and sophomoric, like a guy's. She impersonated minor Canadian celebrities. (Her Brian Linehan rivaled Martin Short's on *SCTV*.) She told Newfie jokes—our equivalent of Polish humor, directed at the good people of Newfoundland. ("How do you kill a Newfie while he's drinking? Slam the toilet seat on his head.") She called people "dinks" and "faggots"—both as insults and terms of endearment. Her idea of an F-word was "Fuzz!" Out of context, none of this sounds sidesplittingly hilarious, but she was very good company.

"You're good for me because I waste all my time entertaining you (something I enjoy very much)," she wrote in one of the letters I dug out of the garage.

At the Douglas Hall Christmas party, we both got very drunk. "Julia's blotto!" the resident Newfie announced. Blotto enough to convert our friendship into the official beginning of a three-year relationship. I lost a friend doing it—she was seeing a Tennessee preppy at the time. But he had to go. This was my first true love.

Dating during our second semester was single-bedded bliss, though I could have done without staring at her Police poster every night. She had a thing for Sting, who according to imdb.com is a full six feet tall.

That summer, she went back to Toronto—our hometown. I went to Oxford, the one in England, to immerse myself in pints of liquid Eng. lit. We wrote impassioned letters. Well, hers were impassioned. Mine were filled with disquisitions on the difference between an "Oxonian" and an "Oxonion." Or so she complains in her letters. I'm sure she was right. I never gave her the mushy romantic stuff she asked for. In letters or in person.

That fall, we shacked up off campus. Oh, the anxiety of those first parental visits when they'd find out we had only—gasp!—one bedroom. We played house in an apartment on Summerhill Avenue, dress-rehearsing for marriage. The cutesy nicknames: "Munchkin," "Rice," and, inexplicably, "Tapir." The scavenger hunt of love notes left around the apartment: "Happy October the 2nd!"—signed with her last name crossed out and mine written in. And, "I love you very much even though you're a faggot sometimes (and I mean a big one)." Another nickname she had for me was "The Minuteman." Hey, I was nineteen! There was chemistry. Sometimes too much.

Our test tube of premature domestication had a tendency to explode. Not just yelling or throwing capons at each other. Actual physical tussles. We were pretty evenly matched, but I could usually take her. Sucking wind, I'd just manage to pin her to the futon like a wrestler, demanding she "give." If we were lucky, the death-match would take a sexy turn. This was, after all, the decade of *Fatal Attraction*. Julia wasn't a bunny-boiler, but she could be a ball-buster. Which was how she was typecast during her college acting career. First, as Lady Bracknell in *The Importance of Being Earnest*, then Martha in *Who's Afraid of Virginia Woolf?*

She got deeper into acting. I got deeper into gunning for a 4.0. The only note I have in my shoe box that's from me to her says, "I've gone to the library, but I'll be back around 11 p.m." What does the "but" mean? Like eleven o'clock was knocking off *early*? In the space of two semesters, I'd gone from a DJ/alcohol-poisoning guy to—as she put it—"developing quite a reputation as a poindexter."

Things started to turn dark. Her notes to me degenerated from "I gotta admit I like living with ya, so always love me, eh?" to "I don't know what's happening to us."

This was after a month.

Another sign of her mounting dissatisfaction was the affair she started having with the gay guy upstairs. Not in the Biblical sense, I'm fairly certain. But I'd come home and find the two of them watching *The Wizard of Oz*, with him prancing around in a pair of her red pumps. This turned out to be another dress rehearsal. Years later, Julia got famous in Canada as host of a cooking show built around her making fun of a short (nowhere near five feet nine) gay sidekick.

I remember how mad she was that I only went one night of the twelve-night run of *Virginia Woolf*. "Term papers" was my excuse. The real reason, I suspect, was I didn't need to sit in the audience when we were living our own George-and-Martha drama every night at home. She was asking more than I could deliver, so I retreated into my books like Albee's toxic marrieds into their booze and bitterness. And, like them, we stayed together anyway.

I graduated. She had a year to go. Five hours I'd drive to visit her from Toronto to Montreal through blinding snow in an ailing Chevette. We'd fight all weekend. It ended, symbolically at least, when I threw up in her best friend's hat. I should mention that I was wasted. And it wasn't a very nice hat. There was no definitive breakup, but the visits stopped. And we were suddenly affectionate in a way unique to that relationship limbo between dating and hating.

"Rickles, I have no one to hug and talk to," she wrote me. "Plus I can't have tantrums because no one notices."

A year after it was over, I tried to get back in there. She rebuffed me. My inability to "open up" was cited. I cursed myself for not being more giving, sensitive, understanding during all those years with her. I consoled myself by hugging tight the belief that I had dumped her.

When I heard her marriage had broken up, I told myself the reason I wanted to reconnect was to offer support. The truth of what I wanted to offer was more like gloating. I never met the now ex-husband but I'd always felt a vague antipathy. When they first started dating, she asked if they could stay at my apartment in New York while I was out of town. I said no. I didn't want my first love and some bouncer-actor-hyphenate soiling my sheets. I might have cast some aspersions on the guy, perhaps invoked the word "freeloader."

Years later, I saw her again and asked if she was "still married." An obnoxious question, even if it proved prescient. Cut to five years ago. She and her husband were renting a house a few doors down from my mother in Toronto. I was home from New York for a visit and Julia drove by. We chatted. She was all smug about being married, having kids, living in Rosedale—it's a fancy neighborhood—while I was still futzing around with a live-in girlfriend (albeit one on the verge of becoming my wife and, later, mother of my children).

When the tabloid news broke that a Canadian B-actor had left his wife for the TV mogul's daughter after a torrid on-set affair, I felt sympathy for Julia—they'd just adopted a second child. And yet some part of me felt vindicated. A little petty rejected voice wanted to say, "You dumped the wrong guy." Which meant deep down I knew all along she'd done it to me. Because if she hadn't, why would I have cared?

When she sent that e-mail, I was certain *she* was the one rewriting history. Then I delved into those musty shoe boxes and found her side of the story. If she has a corresponding archive of my letters, I don't think it would help my cause.

I've always had so much invested in being a dumper, never a dumpee. The motto on the crest of my dating life was, "It's not me, it's you." And usually it was. But there was something liberating about the idea that Julia had dumped me. I lost the urge to gloat. I felt her pain, not the one I'd swept under the rug so many years ago.

"You can be very cruel, like ice, but please not to me, over something so small," said one of those love notes from when we were living together. My friends used to pull her aside to tell her how "good" she was for me, like I was some kind of superdink until she came along. I would normally discount this as a wildly unfair assessment of my personality except my wife says they've told her the same thing.

I hope she doesn't dump me, too.

She Wasn't the One

by Bruce Jay Friedman

Dear Harry [*the letter began*] "You probably won't remember me, but I thought I'd take a chance and write—in the hope that you would. We knew each other in the Long Ago and dated for several months. (My name was Sybil Barnard at the time.) Then we drifted apart. Since that time, I've been married, had two sets of twins, and have recently gotten divorced. ☹

I have followed your career with a great deal of interest—and I thought it might be fun to get together and catch up on old times. I'll be at the Plaza Hotel Nov. 7, 8, visiting my sister, and wonder if you would consider meeting me for a drink. I certainly hope so. If not—I wish you continued good luck—and just write this off as the idle fantasy of an (ex) suburban housewife.

Fondly,

Sybil Barnard Michaels

Harry remembered her, of course. How could he not remember her? He had thought of her for the last twenty-five years, if not every day, then at least once a week for sure. She was The One Who Got Away, or, more correctly, The One Who Broke His Heart and Got Away. She had been a drama student at the University of Colorado. Harry reviewed the plays she was in for the local newspaper. He had dated her during his senior year. She was tall and blonde and beautiful in a quiet regal way, and though Harry was in love with her they had never slept together, which may have been why she broke off their romance so suddenly, and in Harry's view, with such brutality.

Their dates consisted for the most part of the two of them dancing together, along with other couples, in the parlor room of Harry's boardinghouse. At some point in the evening, her skin would become damp and she would start to quiver and say, "Take me home when I feel like this, Harry." And Harry would dutifully and gallantly whip her right back to her sorority house. Whenever they passed the wooded area, where couples slipped off to be together in total privacy, she would say, "Whatever you do, Harry, don't take me in there." And Harry would assure her he had no intention of doing so. They continued along this way, taking walks, seeing an occasional movie together and dancing— less and less dreamily as time went by—in the parlor of Harry's boardinghouse. One night her hand brushed against his erection. She jumped and Harry apologized and told her not to worry, it would never happen again.

In some section of himself, Harry had the sense that all they were doing was treading water. He liked being with Sybil, liked the *idea* of her, but he didn't really know what he was supposed to do next. One night, she asked: "You wouldn't ever consider meeting me in Denver and taking a hotel room, would you?" Harry said of course he wouldn't. This time even Harry knew what she was driving at—but he was twenty years old and had never rented a hotel room before. The thought of walking through the lobby with Sybil and dealing with the desk clerk was more than he could handle. Maybe if she had phrased it differently—or if *she* had arranged for the room.

One night, Harry returned to the boardinghouse after a film course in which the class had dissected *The Loves of Gosta Berling*. Waiting for him at the top of the stairs was his roommate Travis, who was smiling broadly.

"You have a call," said Travis, who must have known what was in store for Harry and was enjoying the moment immensely. He accompanied Harry to the wall booth, as if he were a maitre d', and stood by smartly as Harry picked up the receiver. Sybil was at the other end and wasted no time in telling him that she didn't want to see him anymore.

"I didn't come all the way out here to date just one person, Harry."

He pleaded with her to give him another chance, but she wouldn't budge.

"Maybe after we graduate . . . if you're ever in Charlotte," she said. "But not now."

Harry was sick to his stomach when he hung up, which did not deter Travis from telling him—with enormous pleasure—that Sybil had been dating an agriculture major on the nights she wasn't seeing Harry. Oddly enough, Harry did not hold any of this against Travis. His friend, who was the school's only male cheerleader, had suffered a series of romantic setbacks of his own, all with girls named Mary, and obviously took comfort in having some company.

Harry didn't give up. The next night, he caught up with Sybil, who was on her way to rehearsals for *The Seagull,* and begged her to go out with him one more time.

"I have something to show you," he said suggestively, "that I've never shown you before."

She reacted to this with a little smile, indicating to Harry that the agriculture major had shown her all she needed to see.

He trailed her across the campus, asking her if he could at least have a picture of her for his wallet, but she said she didn't think it would be a good idea.

"Not even a *picture*?" he said, as she disappeared into the rehearsal hall. That seemed awfully cruel to him; spitefully, he made no mention of her in his favorable review of *The Seagull*.

He didn't eat or sleep much in the weeks that followed. To Travis's great delight, he could not even get fried chicken past his throat—the ultimate test of romantic misery. The other fellows in the rooming house gave him lots of room and lowered their voices sympathetically whenever he walked by. One night Harry ran into Sybil's roommate, who looked him over quizzically and said, "You're such a nice man," which really pissed him off.

Soon afterward, Harry recovered slightly and took up with another drama student—from Wisconsin—who slapped her hips against his on their first date and led him into the woods. They made love virtually around the clock, in deserted classrooms, in the library, in the open fields. One result was that Harry came up with the worst case of poison ivy in the history of the school. He had to just lie there in the hospital under a sheet for days at a time. But none of this erased the memory of Sybil.

He saw her only one more time, dancing with the agriculture major at the senior prom, her face close to his, and her fingers on his neck. He was with the Wisconsin drama student, who looked great and was extremely jolly—but it didn't help and he spent the evening with his heart in his shoes.

After he graduated, and in the years that followed, Harry continued to nurse the memory of his loss, like an old football injury. It's entirely possible he got married because of Sally's fairly close resemblance to his first love. Maybe there was more to it, but Harry didn't think so. Thus, you could argue that Harry had had to endure an entire unnecessary marriage and have a child and then get a divorce—all because of Sybil. And she wanted to know if he remembered her.

Strangely enough—and call it ego if you will—Harry had always known that he would hear from Sybil. And maybe even get a letter from her, similar to the one he held in his hand. Each time Harry received a credit on a movie, or even a partial, he wondered if she had noticed his name on the screen. She was out there somewhere; surely she went to the movies. He didn't see how she could possibly have missed his name entirely, particularly in the case of his two big pictures. The letter proved that she hadn't. When she saw his name up there, Harry wondered if she had ever regretted her decision to dump him unceremoniously without so much as a farewell photograph.

Now that he had the letter, he could hardly wait for Julie to get back from the construction site so he could tell her about it. The great thing about Julie is that he could fill her in on an episode like this with no fear of criticism. And he could count on her to enjoy it along with him. They had been living together at the beach for two years now, a couple of hours' drive from the city. Julie was working for the post office when they met and had made a recent switch over to carpentry, which she enjoyed more than delivering mail. Each morning she went off to join her construction crew—a great bunch of guys from Greenport—while Harry stayed behind and worked on the screenplay he was doing for a little Czech company that paid him in cash. He was enormously proud of Julie for going into carpentry. And the look of her in work clothes was a tremendous turn-on. One day he ran into her accidentally at the deli, reading off a sandwich order for the crew from a two-by-four. He had wanted to pull off her bluejeans right on the spot.

When Julie got home around five, Harry said he had something to tell her and she said great, but could he hold on for a minute while she settled in. He said fine and did his best to bide his time while she went to the john, checked the mail, and popped open an Amstel Light. Then she lit a Nat Sherman cigarello and plopped down in a living room chair, with one leg slung over the armrest, and told him to fire away. She did not like to listen to Harry's stories on the fly. Or at least his old ones.

Harry told her about Sybil and the letter and didn't she think he ought to meet her at the Plaza and play it out. Julie didn't agree wholeheartedly, but she did agree a little bit and said that if Harry wanted to meet her he should go ahead and do so. Instead of letting it rest, Harry said it would give the experience some closure, a new term he had picked up from the psychiatrist he had been seeing on and off for several years. Julie said she understood the concept and could see that it would be important for him to have some closure.

"But what if she's gorgeous?" she asked.

Harry had never seen anyone with eyes like Julie's. They could be warm and playful and kind, all at the same time. That and the work boots and the carpentry. Sometimes it was too much for him.

"It's beside the point," said Harry. "That was twenty-five years ago."

"I don't care," said Julie. "And what if she sees your shoulders and tush?"

Harry said she had already seen them, and decided he had to have Julie.

"Now?" she said, in mock panic. "When I haven't even read the *Post*? And I haven't come down from my carpentry?"

"Right now," said Harry.

"Okay," she said with a sigh, and took off her sweatshirt. "But let's not get into a whole big thing."

Harry was understandably jumpy on the day he was scheduled to meet Sybil. Normally, on his trips to the city, he stayed over at a hotel, since he didn't relish the idea of driving back and forth in one day. But on this occasion, he made sure not to book a room, probably as a safeguard against things getting out of hand. Another reason Harry was edgy was that he feared he would see a record of his own aging in Sybil's face. That had happened to a character in an Isaac Bashevis Singer story, who had run into a childhood friend in a railway station, and Harry did not need it happening to him.

As he walked through the lobby, Harry wondered if he would be able to recognize Sybil. He had reserved a table in a dark corner of Trader Vic's, just in case she had gotten fat. Call him a swine if you like, but he was not anxious to be caught having lunch with a fat, older woman. There were several middle-aged women in the lobby who were clearly not her. After fifteen minutes of looking around, Harry started to get irritated and wondered if she had changed her mind and decided not to show up at all. That would put him in the position of having to think about her for another twenty-five years. With no closure. And then she walked up to him—or marched up to him, more accurately— and Harry literally received the shock of his life. She was all furs and pearls and white skin and fragrance and she was far more beautiful than Julie—or Harry, for that matter—had feared.

"Hi, Harry," she said, kissing him on the cheek. "Sorry I'm late."

"That's perfectly all right," said Harry, who was every bit as unsettled as he had been the first time he met her at the sorority house and helped her on with her coat. His choice of Trader Vic's had been a good one, but for another reason. He wanted to be alone with her in the dark setting.

He led her off to the restaurant and after they had settled into the corner booth and ordered Mai Tais, she said he looked exactly the same.

"Maybe a little less hair," she said, after another quick study.

Harry raised one hand to his forehead and felt it was a fair appraisal. Actually, he felt he had gotten off easy.

"And you look fabulous," he said, deciding in his new maturity not to add that she hadn't aged a day. He decided to leave age out altogether.

"I couldn't figure out what to wear," she said. "I thought maybe kneesocks."

"Kneesocks," he said reverentially. The thought of her long slender legs in kneesocks made him dizzy. He wanted to run right off with her and have her put some on for him.

He said it again.

"Kneesocks."

She brought him up to date on her life—her marriage to a developer, the divorce, the twins, the humdrum suburban life, which was obviously no match for what she perceived as Harry's exciting one—and said that one reason she had come to the city was to see if she could find work in the theatre.

"I thought possibly you could help me."

"What kinds of parts would you play?" he asked.

Her face fell and Harry saw that she had taken it the wrong way—or maybe the right way—and he wished he could have taken back the question. As it was, he made a limp effort to paper it over.

"Now that I think about it," he said, "there are all *kinds* of roles you could handle."

She took a little time to recover, but once they were back on track he quickly worked Julie into the conversation, saying they were great friends and had been living together for two years at the beach.

"She's a carpenter," said Harry.

The fact that she and Harry were great friends and that she was a carpenter didn't seem to make much of an impression on Sybil.

"I'm so delighted you remembered me," she said.

Harry was happy to admit that not only did he remember her but that she had rarely been out of his thoughts. And then he couldn't resist reminding her of the sudden and seemingly cruel way in which she had dropped him, without so much as a farewell photograph.

"I *hated* my photograph, Harry," she said. "Surely you didn't expect me to give you a photograph I hated."

Then she lowered her eyes.

"And I was afraid of you then. You were so sophisticated."

All of this was news to Harry. The photograph explanation made sense, but the thought of Harry being sophisticated at twenty—and of someone being afraid of him—was laughable. He wasn't sure how sophisticated he was right that minute.

"I wasn't ready for you then," she added, leaving the impression—unless Harry was way off the mark again—that she just might be ready for him now.

To shore up his man-of-the-world credentials, Harry stretched back and said he had done just about everything. She matched him in the erotic department by saying she had done just about everything herself. Then she cocked her head and thought for a second, as if to set the record straight.

"Except two things."

Harry didn't inquire as to what they were. Why take the risk of having the reunion come to a crashing halt. But he certainly did wonder what the two things were. He guessed that one of them had to do with the backdoor route. As to the second, he didn't have a clue.

"I guess I've been waiting for the right time to do them."

Harry couldn't handle that one at all, so he let it sit for a while. Then she asked him if he was free for dinner. She was meeting her sister and brother-in-law, who was a psychiatrist. The plan was for them to attend a party on Riverside Drive for a woman who was dying. Friends and relatives had been invited to sit around with her, in a party atmosphere, with incense burning, while she continued to die.

"It's a kind of die-in, I suppose," she said. "Would you like to come along? Afterward, we have a reservation at a Thai restaurant."

Harry said that under normal circumstances, he would love to join her, but he had promised Julie he would be home in time for dinner.

She pressed him on it, but he held his ground. And then he paid the check and walked her to the elevator, which took a long time to get there. While they were waiting, she tilted her head up to be kissed, in the sorority style, and Harry took her up on it, not quite getting all of her mouth, no doubt because he was torn twenty different ways. But he felt the length of her, the long legs and the spare chest. Then his hands dropped to the substantial, maybe oversubstantial bottom that didn't quite go with the rest of it—and Harry saw for the first time that it wasn't his youth and inexperience and fear that had kept him from taking her into the woods many years back. The fit wasn't quite right, and it wasn't quite right now. He had probably known it then too, but had preferred to blank it out so that he could hold on to his sweet agony in the years that followed. Still, he enjoyed her fragrance, the freshness of her mouth, the rich feel of her fur coat against his cheek. Harry had been leading a quiet, pleasant life, but there had been something missing, and now he thought he knew what it was.

"Would you like to come up for a drink?" she asked.

He looked at his watch and said he'd love to, but that he had better not.

"I have to get moving if I want to miss the rush hour."

"Well," she said, clearly disappointed, "if you ever get to Charlotte . . . "

He thought about her house and the twins and the way she lived, but he knew he was never going to see any of it. All the same, he told her that if he was ever in the area of Charlotte he would be sure to look her up.

They shook hands, and with her fragrance still trailing after him, Harry headed straight for the gift shop. Because of the kiss he felt he had better pick up something for Julie. He had been struggling with a project that had to do with wood nymphs and, as luck would have it, he found a vanity table mirror that had a wood nymph for a handle. Harry picked it up and was about to bring it over to the sales clerk when he spotted a gossip columnist he knew at the magazine rack. He was all filled up with his recent experience and decided to tell the gossip columnist about it, even though he didn't know her very well.

"You'll never guess what just happened," he said. And then it all came pouring out in a rush, starting with the college romance and his broken heart, the passage of time and then, years later, the letter, all of it culminating in the lunch he'd just had at Trader Vic's. She listened without comment and when he had finished, she pointed to the mirror and said, "That is the tackiest piece of shit I have ever seen."

There was still some daylight remaining when he got home. He went straight up to the bedroom and found Julie curled up on the bed, with a lapful of mysteries, puffing on a Nat Sherman cigarello and working her way through a six-pack of Amstel Lights. In other words, all of her favorite things to do. He wondered how one person could read so many mysteries until one day he caught her skipping ahead and unconscionably peeking at the last page of one.

"So how'd it go, stud?" she asked, not quite taking her eyes off the book she was working on.

"Just fine," he said.

The casual tone made her look up.

"What do you mean by that?"

"What I said," he answered, slinging his coat on top of the jumble of clothing piled up on a chair. "It went just fine."

Harry gave her the gift and when she had unwrapped it she said it was very nice. The lack of enthusiasm didn't bother Harry. It took her a while to warm up to gifts. In another month or so, she would go around saying it was one of the best things she had ever owned.

"Was she gorgeous?"

"In a way," said Harry, popping open one of her precious Amstels.

"In what way was that?" she asked, her interest picking up. And then, with a playful kind of panic, she said, "*Harry,* you didn't *do* anything, did you?"

"How can you ask a question like that?" he said, continuing the game.

And then, before she could get out another one of her queries, with her eyes dancing, he sunk down beside her in the unmade bed in the tangle of beers and mysteries and laundry and cigarettes and bluejeans that was his life whether he liked it or not and hugged her so hard he almost broke her bones. He knew then that he loved her upside down and inside out, fat or skinny, rich or poor, sick, healthy, the whole list. He loved her wet green eyes, the chuckle, her rough hands, the right one extended, palm up, when she wanted to make a serious point. He loved her whiskey voice, her teenage breasts, her crazy hair after a shampoo, and before one, too, and if she didn't want to be buried right next to him, he'd be disappointed, but that would be all right, too, as long as she gave it some serious thought. He wanted her, and if he didn't know it the instant he met her, he knew it ten minutes later. *Her.* The very word made him weak.

He just wished she'd wear a skirt once in a while.

Notes Towards a Unified Theory of Dumping

by Sam Lipsyte

Introduction

What is dumping? Why do people dump other people? Is it because they don't want to be with those people? Is it because they want to be with other people? Is the drive to dump an evolutionary adjustment? Did early man dump? By early man do we mean really hairy man? Hairy like my great-uncle Seymour, or even hairier? These are not idle questions. Just because I am often idle, it doesn't mean you have to drag the questions into it, call them idle, too.

In 1995 I was awarded The McDonnell-Douglas "Smart Guy" Fellowship to continue my work in the fields of Applied Desire and Advanced Biffing. My proposal centered on the notion of a *Unified Theory of Dumping*, an idea first broached by my mentor, Dr. Benny Wallinger, and his research partner, Shem Orsley. Many are doubtless familiar with *The Stanford Dumping Experiment* and the terrible effects it produced in otherwise healthy subject couples. Anybody unfamiliar with those unfortunate events would do well to consult Orsley's account, *The Devil's Data: The Corruption of Benny Wallinger*. Though both scientists died some time ago (Wallinger at the hand of his fifth wife, Gwenda), and all of their research was discredited, the notion of a *Unified Theory of Dumping* continued to haunt me, even during the completion of my major work, *Bifurcations: Penile Duality in a Multivalent World*.

Still, my research remains unfinished, and I fear my empirical powers have begun to wane. Herewith I offer my notes towards a *Unified Theory of Dumping* with the hope that the next generation of scientists will not shirk from the task. Now that global climactic calamity is increasingly difficult to refute, it is imperative that the scientific community develop a workable theory of dumping so we may better understand why our society sucked so bad before it was completely underwater.

I'd be lying if I didn't also admit to a personal stake in this project. Simply put, I am not just an objective observer of dumping phenomena. I have long been a victim of our ignorance of their properties as well. Indeed, had I been born to a future age that better understood dumping, I could have been spared a great deal of suffering. But such was not my fate. Like Galileo and other trailblazers before me, I have martyred myself to a dogged pursuit of the truth, risking penury, calumny, and many other things that end in *y*. But until my dying breath I will endeavor to understand precisely which natural forces colluded to obstruct my happiness.

The following cases are culled from my own experience, and are offered with the expectation that such anecdotal evidence is but the first step in the long march toward a comprehensive knowledge of dumping, a phenomenon I believe may turn out to be closely linked to certain unnamed vixens who, if you'll excuse such a flight of lyrical fancy in a man of science, thrill to heel-stab our trusting hearts like so many crush porn gerbils, and then use the resulting organ paste to rouge their hideous death mask visages. In other words, I hope my notes will help.

Case #25

It was maybe the fortieth time I'd done that fake reach for my wallet in a restaurant. We both knew I didn't have any money. We were very young and not really in love but we liked to drink gin together and watch *Star Trek* reruns and eat nice dinners and later have gin-soaked post-dinner Trekkie sex. She was an extremely elegant woman. I know the *Star Trek* part might make some doubt me, but think of the body and poise required for those uniforms. I'm not saying she wore one. It's not my place to say that.

She was witty and warm. Worst of all, she had money, and I had none. At the time I preferred to view it as "dining out on Star Fleet's tab," but I still wonder what made her buy me a really nice dinner thirty-nine times and then on the fortieth suddenly snap, say, "You know what, I'm sick of you reaching for your wallet like you have any money in it, and I'm sick of buying you dinner and gin and I'm sick of driving you around everywhere, even to go hang out with your friends without me, like you're my kid and you're in kindergarten or something. So I hope you enjoyed that sushi because I'm cutting you off. We're done. We're not going to see each other anymore. And yes, I'll drive you to Steve's house now."

Why did it happen at that dinner and not another? Did it have something to do with the *Star Trek* reruns being on hiatus for a few weeks? Again, there is much to explore, but my scientific hunch is that there may be what can only be called a "tipping point" at work here, by which I mean precisely that: a point where it was incumbent upon me to offer to pay the tip. By my calculations I believe this occurred at dinner #38. Duck confit.

Case #13

Due to reasons I still cannot quantify, it is often the end of a relationship that allows one to register its prior existence. During junior high I was "going out" with a girl who made me put my finger in her all the time. That was our big activity. I didn't even do that much with my finger. We'd stare in each other's eyes and not kiss, and then I'd put my finger in her. She told me to never talk to her around other people.

There was a class trip down to Washington, D.C. It was supposed to be the highlight of the year. The lead teacher on the trip, Mr. Matossian, told us it would be the "greatest experience of our lives." He made it clear that by the "greatest experience of our lives" he didn't mean our lives so far. He meant this would be the peak of our lives, and that everything after this would be pain and disappointment.

We were quite excited. The year before, according to rumors, a boy had been arrested for defacing the Lincoln monument with a turd doodle. The cops, Lincoln fans, beat the boy with phone books. Only because Mr. Matossian had certain contacts in the law enforcement community was the boy released without charges. We were all eager to be beaten with phone books and then rescued by Mr. Matossian. I was also eager to put my finger in the girl the whole day's ride down to Washington. She made a big announcement about how she couldn't believe she had to sit next to a loser like me, but she'd also brought a blanket and as soon as our bus pulled out of the ShopRite parking lot, I went to work. The trip turned out sort of boring, but that was by far the greatest bus ride of my life. Maybe that's all Mr. Matossian meant.

But a strange thing happened afterward, or rather, the next fall, when we attended high school. We suddenly weren't doing that thing with my finger anymore. We lost contact with each other. I asked her what had happened, but she seemed not to hear me. She looked at me as though she'd never seen me before. At first I wondered if I was witnessing the onset of some kind of cognitive dysfunction, but it later occurred to me that, against all scientific probability, or at least in contradiction to my limited sense of these matters, she had been, in fact, using me. After further research, the idea that women sometimes use men, and not just vice versa, became quite apparent to me. Some of this research was personally quite painful, but I'd be lying if I said that, given the chance, I wouldn't conduct my studies all over again. Some pain doesn't hurt at all. It tingles.

Case #17

The preemptive dump, which can only be viewed as an evolutionary defense against the emotional calamity known as rejection, was first brought to my attention by a three-hundred-pound county shot-put champion nicknamed "The Sheik," though I believe he was of mixed Swiss-Swedish descent. The preemptive dump was just a folk tradition at that point, and had not been subjected to the rigors of science, but I immediately saw its potential for widespread, or at least repetitive, application. We were in the locker room after track practice, and The Sheik stood at the mirror pinching great gobs of zit pus from his neck as he explained the process:

"It's always the same, dude. You can see it in her eyes. She's ready to dump your ass. You ask about Saturday night and she says she's not sure. She might have to help her family get ready for her father's wake. That's when you make your move. Tell her it's over. Tell her to get lost. I mean, fuck that shit, right?"

I have initiated the preemptive dump on a few occasions, including once with a college sweetheart we'll call Melissa, though her name was actually Malissa. There are a lot of things I could tell you about Melissa, but suffice to say we were young and I was a boy and she was girl and I had a penis and she had that thing that just wants a penis to be in it immediately. I told her as much and she looked at me oddly. So, thinking of The Sheik's advice, I dumped her ass, whereupon she said, "I don't know what you're talking about, but please step away from my carrel." I winked at her, and silently thanked my tremendous friend.

Case #37

A confession: the numbers I've been assigning these cases are random, or not even random, but designed to make people think I've had more experience than is perhaps, technically, true. Why would I do that? To serve science, that's why. There are no ethics when the truth is on the line, and if I have to lie about how much I've gotten to get people to take my findings seriously, I will not hesitate. Still, do not be mistaken. I have not fared so poorly for a man in my condition.

This case in point, one to tantalize the pure math crowd, takes the form of a problem first advanced by my mentor Wallinger after a few games of racquetball, a long steam, and a half carafe of *aquavit* had, as they say, loosened his tongue.

"Tell me, buddy, how can *a* be lucky enough to be even in the *same fucking equation* as *b*, if *a* can be described as mostly balding with soft furry titties, weird leathery patches on his inner thighs, and horned yellow nails curling from his feet like the claws of some fat, wheezing griffin and *b* stands for the few women you've, sorry, I mean, *a* has been with, nice girls who aren't even desperate teenagers from former Soviet satellite states? I mean, how does that happen ever?"

It's an important question, and it is a shame Wallinger's long-suffering wife, Gwenda, booby-trapped his Rubik's Cube before he could examine it more closely. Until now the best minds have only been able to posit the conjecture that I, or, I mean, *a* must go down on the nice girls for hours and then listen rapturously to endless litanies of their fears and desires, however trifling or superficial.

There is some statistical truth to this, but there are more variables to consider. Some women dig a guy with furry titties. And I am a better-than-average listener. I once listened to a woman describe her relationship with her sister for over an hour. These facts cannot be ignored when advancing a unified theory of dumping, or really, a theory of anything. That shit was boring.

A Case for Further Study

My son was born nearly three years ago. Many are the nights I will return from a grueling day at the lab and he will be there, sitting in my wife's arms. He will stare at me unflinchingly while slipping his hand into my wife's blouse and massaging her breasts. "Go away," he will intone. He was weaned a long time ago. He just likes to feel her up. I am very worried for him, for I do not think he understands that eventually he will be unable to do this, that my wife will, in effect, dump him, disallow these fondles and caresses, much as she was eventually forced to do with Larry, our super, during a confusing time I'm not sure I fully understand. The potential ramifications are quite disturbing, and somehow I can't shake the image of those poor Stanford students all those years ago. Most of them recovered, but a few did not attend top law schools.

It's partly my fault, I know. I should never have had sex with my wife. But I worry for the future of science, and our planet. The time has come for us to put petty grievances aside and join together. We must pool our knowledge for a better understanding of the neurological, ecological, and biochemical effects of dumping in all its forms. We must also explore alternatives to human intimacy. Some of these alternatives will reveal themselves after the scientific method runs its course. Other alternatives, such as being afraid to commit and having a very large dog in your apartment, have been with us forever. All avenues must be explored.

We need a unified theory of dumping and we need it now. Otherwise, we will have learned nothing from the eons of heartbreak our species has endured, and we will remain disastrously unprepared for what promises to be a very complicated dating future, where in all likelihood one's sexual success will depend entirely on the slant of one's gills.

Contributors

Stephen Colbert

Stephen Colbert is the host and executive producer of *The Colbert Report* on Comedy Central.

Marcel Dzama

Winnipeg-born artist Marcel Dzama's art has appeared in hundreds of international exhibitions. In 2006, the IKON Gallery in Birmingham, UK, presented an early career retrospective of his work entitled "Marcel Dzama: Tree With Roots." A collection of his work, *The Berlin Years*, was published by McSweeney's Books in 2003. He has designed CD covers for Beck and the Weakerthans and illustrated a children's book in collaboration with They Might Be Giants. Dzama currently lives and works in New York.

Will Forte

Will Forte has been a cast member on *Saturday Night Live* since 2005. He voiced Abe Lincoln on the series *Clone High* and appeared in the film *Beerfest*. He also wrote and starred in the film *The Brothers Solomon*.

Bruce Jay Friedman

Bruce Jay Friedman was born in New York City in 1930 and started his career as an editor and magazine and short-story writer. Friedman has published eight novels and four short-story collections, as well as a half dozen plays. His screenwriting credits include *Stir Crazy* (1980), *Doctor Detroit* (1983), and *Splash* (1984), which received an Academy Award nomination for Best Original Screenplay. *The Collected Short Fiction of Bruce Jay Friedman*, published in 1997, contains fifty-seven of his stories, and *Even the Rhinos Were Nymphos*, a collection of Friedman's best nonfiction, was published in 2000. *Sexual Pensees*, an erotic memoir, was published in 2006. His newest collection is entitled *Three Balconies*.

Matt Goodman

Matt Goodman graduated from high school in the spring of 2007. He is currently enrolled at Swarthmore College. Goodman was the editor in chief of *Sonny Paine*, a high school literary journal published by 826NYC, a nonprofit writing organization for children. Goodman is also an 826NYC volunteer. Check it out: www.826nyc.org.

Alex Gregory

Alex Gregory has been a *New Yorker* cartoonist since 1999. He lives in Los Angeles and has written for various television shows, including *The Late Show with David Letterman*, *The Larry Sanders Show*, and *King of the Hill*. He has a wife, two daughters, and is an accomplished pilot. The people who harp on the fact that he has never flown a plane or successfully operated a flight simulator are just jealous of his innate flying skills, so if you ever find yourself on a plane he's piloting, just sit back and relax. It's all going to be fine.

Marcellus Hall

Marcellus Hall is an illustrator for publications such as *The New Yorker, The New York Times, The Wall Street Journal,* and *The Atlantic Monthly.* He is a songwriter and musician who, with the bands Railroad Jerk and White Hassle, has released albums and toured North America, Europe, and Japan. More about Marcellus Hall can be found at www.marcellushall.com.

Todd Hanson

Todd Hanson is not only sexy as hell, he is part of one of the most respected comedy voices of his generation, thanks to his central role for nearly two decades now as a writer and editor at *The Onion—America's Finest News Source.* Other than that, he has never accomplished anything in his entire life. He lives in Brooklyn with his two cats, James Boswell and Dr. Samuel Johnson.

Nick Hornby

Nick Hornby is the author of the novels *A Long Way Down, How to Be Good, High Fidelity,* and *About a Boy,* as well as the memoir *Fever Pitch.* He is also the author of *Songbook,* a finalist for a National Book Critics Circle Award, and editor of the short-story collection *Speaking with the Angel.* Hornby is the recipient of the American Academy of Arts and Letters E. M. Forster Award, and the Orange Word International Writers London Award 2003.

A. J. Jacobs

A. J. Jacobs is the author of *The Know-It-All,* a memoir of a year spent reading the Encyclopedia Britannica in its entirety as well as *The Year of Living Biblically,* about his attempt to follow all the rules of *The Bible.* He is the editor-at-large at *Esquire* magazine. He sometimes writes about himself in the third person.

Barbara Karlin

Barbara Karlin was born and raised in New York City. Though she no longer lives there, her heart still resides with the Yankees, the Village, and Fifth Avenue. She currently lives in Boston with her spouse, Linda George. She is the proud parent of three wonderfully interesting and attractive children, any one of whom would be a great catch. She is the grateful owner of two very independent Cairn terriers.

Bob Kerrey

For twelve years prior to becoming president of the New School, Bob Kerrey represented the state of Nebraska in the United States Senate. Before that he served as Nebraska's governor for four years. Educated in pharmacy at the University of Nebraska, Kerrey served three years in the United States Navy. He is the author of *When I Was a Young Man: A Memoir*. In May 2005, Kerrey received the Robert L. Haig Award for Distinguished Public Service from the New York State Bar Association, and an honorary doctor of laws degree from New York Law School.

Damian Kulash, Jr.

Damian Kulash, Jr. is the singer for the rock band OK Go, who's most recent album is *Oh No*. He has won a Grammy, been published in *The New York Times*, gotten arrested on *Disney* property, and ridden an elephant. He lives in Los Angeles with his wife and two dogs.

Sam Lipsyte

Sam Lipsyte's most recent novel is *Home Land*, a *New York Times* Notable Book for 2005 and winner of *The Believer* Book Award. He is also the author of *The Subject Steve* and *Venus Drive*.

His work has appeared in *The Quarterly, Noon, Open City, N+1, Slate, McSweeney's Quarterly Concern, Tin House, Esquire, Bookforum, The New York Times Book Review,* and *Playboy,* among other places. He teaches at Columbia University's School of the Arts.

Rick Marin

Rick Marin is the author of the bestselling memoir *Cad: Confessions of a Toxic Bachelor.* He has also been a reporter at *The New York Times,* a senior writer at *Newsweek,* and a pseudonymous advice columnist on men for a major women's magazine. He and his wife, Ilene Rosenzweig, live in Los Angeles with their two boys, Diego and Kingsley.

Tom McCarthy

Tom McCarthy is an actor, writer, and director. He wrote and directed the BAFTA and Independent Spirit award-winning *The Station Agent,* as well as the soon to be released film, *The Visitor.* He has appeared in such films as *Meet the Parents, Good Night and Good Luck, Syriana,* and *Flags of Our Fathers,* as well as HBO's *The Wire.* He lives in New York.

Jason Nash

Jason Nash is a writer, actor, and comedian. He is also the creator and cohost of the comedy podcast *Guys with Feelings* (guyswithfeelings.com). Nash was a cast member of the VH1 sketch show *Random Play* and has appeared on Comedy Central's *Reno 911* and *The Andy Dick Show.* He is a cast member on Comedy Central's *Lil' Bush* and also provides writing and voices for the animated shows *Supernews* and *The Superficial Friends.* Jason lives in L.A. with his wife, son, and dog Hudson.

Bob Odenkirk

Bob Odenkirk has written for *Saturday Night Live, The Ben Stiller Show, Get a Life,* and numerous other TV shows and pilots. He created and starred in *Mr. Show*, which ran on HBO for four years. He also produced and directed the series *Derek and Simon: The Show* for the website SuperDeluxe.com. He has directed the feature films *Melvin Goes to Dinner*, *Let's Go to Prison*, and most recently *The Brothers Solomon*.

Patton Oswalt

Patton Oswalt is an actor, stand-up comedian, and writer who has appeared in shows such as *Reno 911* and *The King of Queens*. He also provided the voice of Remy in the 2007 film, *Ratatouille*.

Neal Pollack

Neal Pollack is the author of *Alternadad*, a best-selling memoir in which he reveals that parenthood will not stop him from being a grumpy stoner. He's also written three books of satirical fiction, including the cult classic *The Neal Pollack Anthology of American Literature* and the rock 'n 'roll novel *Never Mind the Pollacks*, and he's edited *Chicago Noir*, a book of short crime fiction. Pollack's fiction, nonfiction, humor, and essays have appeared in every English-language publication except for *The New Yorker*, and he also writes for about a hundred websites. If that wasn't enough to make you fall in love with him, he's also one of the creators of *Offsprung*, an Internet community and humor magazine for parents or people who might someday be parents. Pollack lives in Los Angeles with his wife, Regina Allen, his son, Elijah, and his dogs, Hercules and Shaq.

David Rees

David Rees is an artist and writer whose comics include *My New Fighting Technique Is Unstoppable*, *My New Filing Technique Is Unstoppable*, and *Get Your War On*, which appears in *Rolling Stone*.

Andy Richter

Andy Richter went to film school and studied improvisational comedy in Chicago. He television credits include *Late Night with Conan O'Brien*, *Andy Richter Controls the Universe*, and *Andy Barker P.I.*, among others. His films include *Elf*, *Talledega Nights*, *Semi-Pro*, and a few without Will Ferrell. He lives in Los Angeles with all those other assholes.

Rodney Rothman

Rodney Rothman is the author of *Early Bird: A Memoir of Premature Retirement*. He is the former head writer of *The Late Show with David Letterman*. He was also a writer on Fox's *Undeclared*. He has contributed to *The New York Times*, *The New Yorker*, *The Best American Non-Required Reading*, *McSweeney's Quarterly Concern*, and *Men's Journal*.

Dan Savage

Dan Savage is the author of the nationally syndicated advice column *Savage Love*. His books include *The Kid*, *The Commitment: Love, Sex, Marriage and My Family*, and *Skipping Towards Gomorrah*. He lives in Seattle.

Adam Schlesinger

Adam Schlesinger is a songwriter as well as the bassist for the band Fountains of Wayne, whose albums include *Utopia Parkway*, *Welcome Interstate Managers*, and *Traffic and Weather*. Schlesinger has written songs and composed music for films such as *That Thing You Do!* and *Music and Lyrics*.

Andy Selsberg

A long time ago, Andy Selsberg was a staff writer at *The Onion*. More recently, he has written for *The Believer*, *GQ*, and *The Oxford*

American. He teaches English at the City University of New York and lives with his wife, Izzy, and a troublemaking cat.

Tom Shillue

Tom Shillue often performs stand-up in front of large crowds of laughing people. You've probably seen him in lots of TV commercials. He's had his own Comedy Central stand-up special, and his live comedy CD, *Overconfident*, could probably be found at iTunes or his eponymous website.

Paul Simms

Paul Simms is a writer and director. He created the show *NewsRadio* for NBC and has also written for *Late Night with David Letterman* and *The Larry Sanders Show*. Simms has also contributed pieces to *The New Yorker.*

Eric Slovin

Eric Slovin is a writer and comedian in New York. As half of the comedy team Slovin & Allen he has made many television appearances including a half hour *Comedy Central Presents*. He worked for three seasons as a writer for *Saturday Night Live.*

Dan Vebber

Milwaukee native Dan Vebber served His Country as one of the first editors of *The Onion* before writing for *Space Ghost Coast to Coast, Daria, Futurama, American Dad,* and other such programs catering to the valuable stoned-kids-who-light-their-farts demographic. He currently resides in Development Hell, where his projects include a stapled, Xeroxed packet of his cartoons rejected by *The New Yorker*, due to be sent to his mother sometime in '08.

David Wain

David Wain is a director, writer, comedian, and actor. He co-wrote and directed the movies *Wet Hot American Summer* and *The Ten*. On television he co-created and starred in two series: *The State* for MTV and *Stella* for Comedy Central. He lives and works in New York and on www.davidwain.com.

Larry Wilmore

Emmy Award winner Larry Wilmore has been working in television for nearly twenty-five years as a stand-up comedian, actor, writer, and producer. He is currently the "Senior Black Correspondent" (after a brief stint as "Black Correspondent") on *The Daily Show with Jon Stewart* on Comedy Central. He has also most recently been a consulting producer on *The Office* on NBC, where he has also appeared as a performer. Wilmore was also creator and executive producer of *The Bernie Mac Show* for Fox, for which he won an Emmy, an NAACP Image Award, and a Peabody; as well as executive producer and co-creator of *The PJs* starring Eddie Murphy. He is currently writing his first book.

Acknowledgments

Honestly, I decided to do an anthology because I thought it would be easier than writing a whole book by myself. I was wrong. Compiling this was never easy and I was an idiot for thinking it would be otherwise. That is my first and foremost acknowledgment. I am dumb.

That being said, many people contributed in ways great and small to make this book happen. Comparatively, a relative few made it much, much harder. They will be getting their own acknowledgment in my follow-up project, *You're Dead to Me*. It will not be funny at all.

First and foremost, I would like to thank each contributor for their time, good will, and most of all for lending their prodigious talents to this project. The best people are usually the busiest, yet the collective *you* made time for this. And not half-assed time. Real time. I sincerely thank you.

By far the person I would like to thank the most is Lauren Sarver. She has been dedicated, professional, diligent, good-humored, and 100 percent reliable. I hope they clone her, ethics be damned. Andy Selsberg is a gifted editor, a talented humorist, a great friend, and oddly, a skilled draftsman. All but one of those came into play during our time working together on this.

Jenn Joel provided many hours of support, counsel, and feedback—all of them useful. Same for Wendy Kirk, who is a spectacularly kind and patient human being. Also, she's great at her job. Lisa Leingang is awesome and helped far more than she thinks she did. I would like to also thank Paul Sahre for his eleventh-hour design wizardry. I almost ruined his trip to France and he was still very nice to me.

David Miner, Cliff Gilbert-Lurie, and Jennifer Fiore brought insight and expertise and the ability to explain what the hell things mean to me. Thank you for that. Also thanks to Leslie Maskin and Sue Naegle for their perpetual support. Mandy Beckner and Will Reiser at Superego came in toward the end, yet still helped me improve this book tremendously.

At *The Daily Show*, giant kudos to Hillary Kun, who is the best at an impossible, often thankless job. Thank you. Also thanks to Kahane Corn, Jen Flanz, David Javerbaum, Rich Korson, Beth Shorr, and Jon Stewart. At *The Colbert Report*, thank you to the unmatchable Meredith Bennett, Rich Dahm, Hilary Siegel, and Allison Silverman.

To Bob Castillo, Jimmy Franco, Ben Greenberg, Sharon Krassney, Anne Twomey, Sara Weiss, and most of all Jamie Raab at *Grand Central Publishing*: I could not ask for a better environment in which to work. Seriously, I am contractually prohibited from asking for a better environment. I should probably not agree to that next time around. Doesn't matter, there isn't one anyway. Thank you.

For their friendship and guidance thanks to Josh Bycel, Izzy Grinspan, Julia Hoffmann, Aaron Lubarsky, Sarah Vowell, Paula Scher, and Stuart Zicherman. Stu's patience is a wonder of the world, like, right next to the Hanging Gardens of Babylon.

To my mom, my dad, Nanci, Lin, Julie, and David, if I've never said thank you for all your love and support over the years, then this is a pretty lame place to first do so. Hopefully, I have and this is just more like a public proclamation of something you all already know . . . right?

And finally, to Paola Guastini, *te amo*.